C000061240

THE
NO B.S.
SMALL
BUSINESS
BOOK

THE
NO B.S.
SMALL
BUSINESS
BOOK

HOW TO WIN WHEN MOST FAIL

CASEY GRAHAM

HOUNDSTOOTH
PRESS

THE NO B.S. SMALL BUSINESS BOOK
How to Win When Most Fail

ISBN 978-1-5445-2408-5 *Hardcover*
 978-1-5445-2406-1 *Paperback*
 978-1-5445-2407-8 *Ebook*
 978-1-5445-2409-2 *Audiobook*

To Kacie, my wife:
your grace saved my life

To Darby, my daughter:
your heart stole mine

To Gage, my son:
your spirit mentors me

CONTENTS

Chapter 0.1

SKIP THIS PART

A.k.a. The Introduction They Made Me Do

The dreaded book introduction. Hard to write. Easy to skip.

If this was a typical business book, I'd tell you to skip reading this. In fact, I wanted to completely skip writing this.

When I was told I had to write it, my first thought was, *Who on earth is going to read this?* followed immediately by, *Why should anyone care?*

Honestly, I'm still not convinced you should read this. I'm still not convinced you should care. But I'm going to give it my best shot anyway. Because if this book truly is all about no B.S., about winning when others fail, then I am going to cut to the chase and get to the why—why you should read this. Why you should care.

Here's a hint: it has nothing to do with me. In fact, it has everything to do with **you**.

BUSINESS BOOKS ARE B.S.

Business books are *full of it*. (You know what I mean by *it*.)

If you want to read fluffy stories and be inspired by motivational quotes, there are plenty of options out there. Knock yourself out. If you are looking for a typical business book that will help you grow and become massively successful while staying devoid of all purpose, save yourself the time by closing this book now.

(In fact, you can return it straight to me if you grabbed the hard copy: P.O. Box 2992, Cumming, GA 30028.)

I'm not going to tell you how to do business, although there will be plenty of takeaways. In fact, I'll tell you more stories about how *not* to do business, with plenty of takeaways.

Look, I'm going to shoot it to you straight. I'm going to be raw, real, and honest, but not for the shock factor—for the no-B.S. factor.

As for you, if you're here for no B.S., then let's get to it. Let's start by making a commitment to not lie to yourself as you read the pages ahead.

Don't lie to yourself, and don't lie to your team.

The people around you want raw, real, and honest leadership. The only way to provide that is by getting raw, real, and honest with yourself. That includes coming face-to-face with what you want *from* your business and what you want *in* your business—and what you *don't*.

As you commit to being raw, real, and honest, I'm going to commit to it too.

We are going to get down to business. We are going to break through the B.S. and get into the business of winning and the business of failing.

So go ahead. Borrow my successful experiences, and try on my massive failures.

When you live and learn vicariously through someone else who has been there and done that, you can skip the Epic Failures line at Disney World for a FastPass into the Magic Business Kingdom of No-B.S. Success.

WHAT YOU WILL LEARN

I am supposed to break it down and tell you exactly what you will get out of this book. I get it. You need to know if the investment of time will be worth it. But here's the deal: only you can decide what you will actually get out of this book, no matter what I promise you.

Still, I am all for clarity and no B.S. (I am also all for not pissing off my editor.) So here are a few things you can expect to learn:

- How to get ruthlessly honest about yourself, your business, and what you *really* want.
- How to create a one-sentence statement that will inform all your business decisions.
- How to think through and execute on those decisions as the owner—not the operator.
- How to structure your business for *your* ultimate satisfaction.
- How to hire to create a company culture that outlasts you.

- How to center each role in your business around *results*—not *activity*.

You'll also learn a ton of in-the-weeds, practical business strategies you can execute tomorrow, including:

- Setting up company rituals.
- Getting crystal clear on your Vision, Mission, and Purpose.
- Establishing Core Values.
- Promoting well.
- Structuring levels of management on your org chart.
- Being financially transparent.
- Building company rituals.
- Hiring (and firing) well.

Overall, this book will help you gain *massive traction* by achieving *massive clarity* as you take *massive action* at all levels of business and life as you approach business and life as a real, raw, and honest No-B.S. Business Owner.

THE NUMBER ONE RULE OF USING THIS BOOK

The only rule in reading this book is that there are no rules. In fact, this book is a raw tale of:

1. How I've royally screwed up.
2. How I'm trying to make up for it.

As such, each part reads well in order, but you can also take nuggets here and there. I hate rules, so I don't want to give you any.

There's incredible freedom and value in consuming this book in the way that best suits you. You have complete permission to:

- Flip to a chapter that sounds interesting.
- Digest a section here or there.
- Read in order.
- Read out of order.

But whatever you do, be sure to not skip the ending. Because the ending is truly just the beginning.

It's the beginning of massive freedom, massive clarity, and massive success that only comes when you are massively clear about *who you are* more than what you do.

If you want to be another owner who is driven by getting rich, I'm not going to judge you. I don't blame you.

In fact, I was you.

Now I know there's a better way to win when most fail, drive massive business results, and be fulfilled in the process.

Let's get down to business.

Chapter 0.2
IT ISN'T YOU
An Apology to Everyone Who Hates Me

Now that you know both how and why you should read the pages ahead, I want to fill in a gap on one last piece: the who.

No, not the band. Specifically, who the hell do I think I am to write a no-B.S. book about small business?

Glad you asked. I'm asking the same question as I pour myself a pint and bust out a cigar.

Allow me to introduce myself along with this disaster of a chapter. (Fair warning: you may want to pour yourself a drink, too. Go ahead. I'll wait.)

My name is Casey Thomas Graham. Thomas came from my granddaddy. They called him Tommy; I called him Papa.

Papa owned a local poultry store called Teagues Poultry when I was growing up. My mom worked there, and she called me every day to ask me what I wanted from the store.

My favorite request was a pickle and Dr. Pepper. I can still taste it. My second favorite was the fried chicken the deep fryer lady, Patsy, made for me.

This business didn't go as planned for Papa.

To make a long story short, he got in over his head financially and shot himself in the chest in the front yard.

As I write this, I'm crying. I'm crying because I'm still mad at him. Rather, I'm still mad about the situation.

I remember seeing him in the coffin before they closed it. I remember not understanding. My twelve-year-old brain was asking, *Why would you do this to us? To me?*

My first exposure to business ownership was a suicide.

This is important. Because when it comes to winning where others fail in business, you'll understand why I know to my core that there's winning, and then there's *winning*. Just like there's failure. And then there's *failure*.

(My failure barometer measures in tears. Ironically, so does my success one. More on that in a minute.)

But first, fast-forward twenty-four years.

I was sitting in Starbucks with my best friend, Richard, and confessing I had thoughts like Papa (yes, those thoughts).

I didn't actually want to kill myself, but I could understand how the darkness creeps in. I was living it.

Richard looked at me straight in the eyes and said words I'll never forget: "You are safe. I love you."

It's powerful to have another human hear your darkest thoughts and *love you anyway*. Especially when you feel incapable of being loved, which is where I sat in that moment.

Maybe Papa never had anyone tell him, "I love you." At least not when he needed to hear it.

I was at my lowest point in that Starbucks with Richard. I had really messed up my life.

In 2008, I started my first company. I was so focused on being successful that I neglected relationships, burned friendships, and screwed over some people.

It reminds me of this leader I knew one time.

Some years after I met him, he wrote a book explaining his perspective on how things were in his organization versus the reality of how his staff saw it. His staff all ordered copies, took screenshots, and laughed at how distorted this leader's reality was compared to what the staff had experienced.

So because of this leader, I vowed if I ever wrote a book, I would just call it like it is. I wouldn't hide behind the print on these pages. In fact, I was going to say I was sorry to all the people on the other side of my mess.

If you're reading this and I fired you, at least some portion of it was my fault.

I'm sorry.

If you're reading this and felt like I was greedy in a negotiation, I probably was. I've been a horrible person at times and let my pride get the best of me.

I'm sorry.

If you're reading this and I screwed you over relationally in some way, I do not expect you to forgive me or even want to talk to me again.

Listen, I will sit down with you and let you tell me all the stupid crap I did, and I will not say anything but...

I'm sorry.

Because I truly am. I'm sorry.

I don't write this as a blanket apology. I write this as a personal invitation to anyone I've screwed over to say, "I'm open to having a meeting."

Some people say, "I would not change anything about my life. It made me who I am."

That's B.S. for me.

I would change a lot. If I could reduce the damage of my stupid leadership and life decisions, I would. Yesterday.

Here's the deal about leadership and life: *there is always blood on the ground when you mix people and money.*

Bad decisions are made. Motives are hard to measure. People hurt people. But I truly believe that the company I co-founded, Gravy Solutions, has become my chance to redeem myself. To redeem my mess. To redeem my tears.

To redeem Papa.

I'll still mess up. But man, I sure do want to live the second half of my life better than the first half. And one of the things I've learned we must do as leaders is genuinely acknowledge our mistakes and take 100 percent ownership of them.

I blame nobody but myself. I challenge you to do the same.

In fact, you committed to not lie to yourself earlier, right? Well, your challenge starts *now.*

As we journey through this book together, know I approach this with a lot of scars and a lot of tears. The keyboard is going to need to be mopped after the wounds that I've wept over as I type this.

And you know what? It's okay to cry. It's okay to shed tears, both in business and in life (I had no idea it would be this cathartic to write this).

My failures are full of tears, and so are my successes. Tears and B.S. can't seem to coexist in my world. So I embrace the tears. Maybe by the end of this book you'll embrace yours too.

Hopefully, you know me a little better now. Hopefully, you've gleaned a spark of insight into the mess that once defined my life.

But hopefully, you'll also see that I'm here with an open heart and battle-scarred hands to just share some things I've learned along the way—things that will help you win where others, especially I, have failed—as you accelerate your life and business.

But first, let's meet Darby and Gage.

It's about to get mushy, squishy, and lovey-dovey for a business book.

I know what you must be thinking: *Didn't I buy a business book? What are all these personal emotions and story lines all about?*

Well, when you are taking your last breath on this earth, you aren't going to ask for your profit and loss statements to surround your bedside.

When you experience pain, you want *people*. We are humans, and our lives affect other humans. We can't forget that. So this business book is written through a *human* lens.

I promised you'd get the real, raw, and honest reflections. This is going to be as real, raw, and honest as I get as I talk about the two most important humans I know: Darby Gail Graham, my daughter, and Gage William Graham, my son.

As you can imagine, they hear a lot from me a lot of the time. They can always take it or leave it with regards to what I tell them. But I hope they will take this for what it's worth.

To Darby and Gage:

If you ever read this book, know that I love you no matter what, no matter who you become—no matter who you don't become. I'm writing this so maybe you can avoid some of the mistakes I've made. I'm also writing this so maybe you can have a head start in your career.

I don't care what you want to be when you grow up. I only care that you find what lights the passion inside your hearts.

In my attempt to find that passion, through success and money, I've found my heart empty. The only thing that truly moves my heart is living in service to other humans.

That's why the premise of our culture at Gravy, the culture you love, is that "everything is an excuse for relationships." My best friend, Louie, said this. And he's right. Business isn't for business's sake; it's for people.

Whatever you do or wherever you end up, Darby and Gage, the purpose is people. *Your résumé won't be read at your funeral.* But I bet people will tell stories about you. What kind of stories do you want them to tell? This book is here to help you answer that question.

Kids, I love you.

—Dad

To you, reader:

These questions aren't just for my kids. They are for you, too.

One day, we will all be nearing the end. (Like tears, death and B.S. can't seem to coexist either.)

You don't have to wait until the end of your life to realize you never became the person you wanted to be. In business. In life.

This won't happen by accident or by chance. In order to win where others fail—in business and in life—you have to commit to getting rid of the B.S. garbage other books and gurus have been feeding you about getting rich, which always comes at the expense of other people.

Because getting rich in business and being successful in life are two widely different things. Yet, when done the right way, they actually can coexist. You can have the business success you want while also having the life you want.

You can win where others have failed, and this book will be your no-B.S. guide to help you achieve *what you really want*.

Some chapters will be heavier than others. Consider yourself warned. But all chapters will be useful for cutting through the crap and getting you where you really want to go while becoming who you really want to be.

The journey starts with one question: what stories will be told about you at your funeral?

Start thinking about that now. The final exam will be at the end of the book.

But first, let's start with taking one single step. Specifically, the single step you need to take to not allow your business to screw up your life.

Are you ready?

Remember: no B.S. allowed.

PART 1

NO-B.S. OWNER'S INTENT

*"Nothing is ever enough when what
you are looking for isn't what
you really want."*

—Arianna Huffington

There's something powerful about knowing what you want. What you *really* want.

However, most of us struggle to get there. You can tell me all day long what you *don't* want, but when it comes to what you want —what you really, *really* want—there's often a lack of clarity and confusion.

Someone trying to be nice has probably told you, "It's not your fault." This failure or that one can be traced back to someone else or something else.

Well, I hate to break it to you: not getting or going after what you want is your fault. At least it will be after you read this part and don't take action.

Discover what you really, really want out of your business and your life and learn what drives you. It's up to you to reach out and take it, starting with crafting *one sentence* built around this core desire.

In this part, we'll dive into the why and the how to make this elusive desire a hard-core reality that sits in the driver's seat.

The result? A more successful business and a much more fulfilled you.

THE SINGLE STEP TO NOT LETTING YOUR BUSINESS SCREW UP YOUR LIFE

An aspiring entrepreneur hired me to be his CEO coach. We spoke often, and every few months I asked him, "What's your Owner's Intent?"

That's fancy for asking, "What do you *really* want?"

I asked that question often because he was a waffler.

- One month, he wanted to scale his business to $10 million.
- The next month, he wanted a lifestyle business.
- The next month, he just wanted to be a bestselling author.

It became apparent that he was missing a crucial ingredient for not just creating success but creating *anything*. He was too close to his business. He couldn't *see* it.

Nobody can really see their own stuff. Nobody can see their deepest problems. As you'll see, I was late to the game myself.

Learning how to do this is a huge step in the direction of winning at business and in life because it's a step where others often fail.

But since it's really easy to see what's wrong with someone else, I let him waffle. He was always changing his mind, so I gave him conflicting suggestions every time we spoke.

After about six months, he got frustrated and said, "Casey, I'm paying you all this money, and you keep changing your advice!" Finally, he'd caught on.

"Because," I gently responded, "every couple of months you tell me you want something different. Until you know *why* you own your business—what it means to your life—and exactly what *you* want out of it, I can't help you."

Call it harsh. I was real, raw, and honest. (No B.S. allowed, right?)

Then, like Obi-Wan Kenobi giving up the fight to Darth Vader, I stopped swinging my lightsaber and said, "You should fire me."

He did.

Zaaaaap!

By letting him fire me, I also became more powerful than he could ever imagine. Because after a few weeks, he called me and said, "I've never understood what you mean by the Owner's Intent.

But now I get it. Until the *owner* knows what he wants, the *operator* can't give it to him."

Bingo.

So who's the operator?

Same guy.

Most business owners and operators are the same person. Certainly at the beginning. And this gets them very messed up. One day, they're thinking at thirty thousand feet, and the next day they're thinking through the weeds.

The owner doesn't know who they are, and they forget the job they should be doing under the mind-bending responsibilities. They never calm down to answer definitively *why* they're doing any of it. Why they're "doing" business.

Because when you're the owner, you want to *change the world.* And when you're the operator, you simply want to order *takeout.*

Get it?

Owners and operators have totally different agendas. Simply put, they absolutely *cannot* be the same person.

That's why *not knowing what you want* as the owner is one of the primary reasons most businesses don't work. Without a strong *why*, your operator self will take over because operations are how you stay afloat.

Your operator self will fire your wishy-washy owner self and proceed to work you to the bone.

Crazy, right?

While I don't have the hard stats to back this up, I have had hundreds of conversations with owner-operators.

I suspect 98 percent of the business owner-operator's thoughts, learnings, and actions center around *running* the business—not *owning* the business. They're working on goals that have *nothing* to do with *why* they started.

Most of the frustrations business owners face are because the operation doesn't give them what they *want*. What they *really* want.

Rarely do people take the time to create what I call Owner's Intent. I wish I could take credit for this term, but I can't. My friend Brian can. My mentor introduced me to him. Brian took a company from $2 million in sales to nearly $1 billion.

I flew to Dayton, Ohio, once to meet Brian and learn from him. I was also looking for funding. After seeing my ridiculous slide deck, he said, "You have no idea how to be an owner." That's not exactly what he said, but it's what I heard.

Over some brisket and pulled pork, he took pity and offered to meet with me and Renee, my co-founder and business partner-in-crime for eighteen years. You will meet Renee many times throughout the book. Without her, I would probably be homeless and smoking crack. To this statement, she will say, "OMG, you're so extreme." (But it's *true*.)

Brian and I fought tooth and nail in a coworking space for eight hours while Renee patiently let us duke it out. I kept wanting to talk about the business. But this successful leader kept saying, "I don't care about your business. Until you know your Owner's Intent, nothing else matters."

Owner's Intent?

"Casey, why do you own this business, and what is your intention with the business? Is it to be a lifestyle business with high profit? Is it to be the next tech unicorn? Is it to grow it and sell it? Five years from now, *what do you want out of the business?*"

I didn't know. I couldn't answer.

"Why" is a hard question because it feels impossible to answer. Your reptile brain questions everything: "How can I know the future?" and "What if I pick wrong?"

It took me about sixty days and a lot of conversations with my wife, Renee, and the Holy Spirit of Gravy, Joe. (Now there is someone I could write an entire book on. Maybe I will one day.)

Finally, after two months, I was able to develop my Owner's Intent for Gravy. Even though Gravy is a payment recovery solution for recurring revenue companies, my Owner's Intent puts so much more value into what Gravy is really for.

Here is my Owner's Intent, word for word:

> *To build a company my adult kids would want*
> *to work at someday if they so choose.*

This one statement is my Owner's Intent. It changed my life. (Thanks, Brian.)

MORE POWER TO YOU

Before you skim over this and say, "Give me the sales hacks, Casey," realize that nothing is more ninja than what I'm about to show you. Answer this question in one sentence. Do it instantly, without thinking about it. If you can, it's like snatching the rock from my open palm: you'll graduate from this book and can buy me a beer.

The question: what do you *really* want?

Tough, right? (Remember, it took me sixty days to find mine, and that's *after I started trying*. Thirty-five years in total.)

The simplicity of a well-thought-out, one-sentence answer that guides you and all your business decisions is powerful. More powerful than you ever will believe.

We start getting power when we know what we want and proclaim it simply. I started to feel this power when I realized I wanted to focus on building a company, over a period of five to ten years, where my kids would want to work.

That's why we only hire 0.02 percent of all the people who apply. And these people? Well, they are top-notch, A-plus players. Yet my filter is the same: would I want my adult children to work with (or for) this person one day?

Because they might.

My Owner's Intent even filters:

- What hotel should we stay at for our Annual Summit? (What happens in Vegas stays in Vegas. And I want to *know* what's going on with my kids. So no Vegas.)

- Who should I speak with about someone who is consistently late? (Because if they're late, my kids will be speaking to this same person.)
- How fast should we grow? (You become sensitive to working people too hard when you're thinking about how you'll navigate spending time with your grown children if they are always working.)

All of these are important questions that now have easy answers because my filter is clear.

Having a clear Owner's Intent will remove 80 percent of your angst.

FULL CIRCLE

Recently, I revisited the conversation with our waffling CEO friend who fired me. He decided *not* to grow his business. Instead, he reduced his staff. Today he's ghostwriting for people.

Through developing his Owner's Intent of doing what he loves—writing books—he is happier and more fulfilled than ever before.

MORAL

Having an Owner's Intent isn't about becoming a billionaire; it's about *making a decision to live your unique life based on what you want.*

In fact, it's the single most important step to keep your business from screwing up your life.

But *why* is it so hard to create? Why do so few owners know *why* they own their business?

I'll tell you why: pornography. Yep, porn gets the best of us.

In fact, you aren't going to want to miss the next chapter.

P.S. For the owners: Tell your operator brain to cool it. Right now it's screaming at you to just get to the business hacks. But trust me: the hacks work 100 percent better when you know your Owner's Intent.

P.P.S. For the team members: What if you aren't a business owner? You might not even own a department or division, but you definitely *own your career*. I would suggest you start reciting this as a mantra: "I may not own the company, but I own *my* part of the company." This will help you determine your career pathway. Plus, you will be more successful the minute you decide to act like an owner and cut through the B.S. once and for all.

BUSINESS PORN BINGE

And Why Watching It Makes You Unsatisfied with Your Reality

You don't have to tell me your dirty little secret. I already know, and I have one to share with you.

We both love porn. *Business Porn.* Don't pretend you don't know what I'm talking about.

It's the steady stream of sensational success stories on LinkedIn, Crunchbase, Forbes, *Entrepreneur* magazine, *The New York Times*, *The Wall Street Journal*, CNN, *Shark Tank*—it's Virgin, SpaceX, Amazon, Apple, Facebook—the lifestyles and accomplishments of Branson, Musk, Bezos, Jobs, and Zuckerberg.

We all freakin' *want* it.

And the media knows it. So they pump out a steady stream of Business Porn to turn us into *The Walking Dead* entrepreneurs, craving another hit of *hustle.*

Now we wake up to Business Porn in emails, newsletters, and podcasts. A constant bombardment of company owners experiencing massive growth and huge revenue.

Mountains of money. "Disruption!" Markets dominated. Owners reveling in the financial windfall of the company sale.

It's all Business Porn.

Business Porn may feed some primal appetite, but I hate to break it to you: it's not real life. It's the B.S. crap most business books and gurus are made of. The danger of Business Porn is that it seeds a false expectation in your mind.

I spoke to a frustrated business owner. She had tried so many different strategies and tactics to make her business grow at pornographic levels. Ultimately (inevitably!) she wasn't satisfied with her results.

"I have to get to $10 million in revenue," she said. "I just have to!"

"Why?" I asked. "What will $10 million in revenue do for you?"

She couldn't tell me.

It was an arbitrary number that wasn't attached to a personal goal or endgame. Somewhere along the way, a steady diet of Business Porn had planted this big *Playboy* centerfold number in her head. It was nothing but a fantasy notion of what success looks like. She was chasing it like she was Hugh Hefner.

Ten million dollars is not a realistic goal. Not because you can't make it but because you *don't know why* you are trying to make it.

▪ She had no idea why her business existed.

- She didn't know what she wanted.
- She did not have an Owner's Intent.

She was pursuing our culture's idea of Business Porn success without a properly oriented internal compass.

Let me put this another way: what do you get when you cross an owner with a headless, flaming chicken? That's right. You get an owner running around like a headless, flaming chicken.

This is a *visionary arsonist*, a term coined by a business coach of mine.

A visionary arsonist is someone who is constantly picking up new ideas from articles, podcasts, and conferences (often written and produced by those same B.S. gurus and business pornographers), implementing them, and then burning all the work down as soon as the next new idea slinks along.

It's like trying to become something that looks right on the outside without figuring out what's actually right on the inside.

THINKING INSIDE THE "BOX"

I met a local gym owner who was having a bunch of success with his "box" (this is lingo for "gym"). He is a wonderful person and an incredibly savvy business owner.

One day after class, we talked about his business.

"Why don't you just grow this thing to three hundred memberships and sell it?" I said. "The economy is great, and you could make a killing and still work out there without the hassle!"

I thought it was a genius move, but I was just a Business Porn zombie. He, on the other hand, was an enlightened owner, and said, "Casey, I don't want to do that. I own the gym because I love the community. My number one priority is to become the number one weightlifter in my age division in the world. I use this gym for that and happen to make money off of it."

Wow.

I was trying to implement *my* Owner's Intent on him, but *he* wasn't having it because he was clear, decisive, and, frankly, more content than I had ever been to that point.

No one writes about the company that makes $500,000 in sales. For sure, no one heaps praise on the gym owner who makes $200,000—even though he's happy, has plenty of free time, and is able to pick his kids up from school every day.

He's living the life *he* always dreamed of living, but his story is just not all that exciting for a media headline.

That's not Business Porn. That's just plain old *success*. The good tears kind of success.

BUSINESS PORNHUB

Let's face it: the companies we celebrate in business—the Business Pornhubs—tend to be huge and make massive revenue. I'm irate about this because I've seen behind the scenes into these ivory towers of success, and often they're filled with a lot of broken people doing some nasty things.

Look inside any of these "hubs" and you're sure to find the skeletons of destructive relationships. You can say, "Can't hurt me," all day, but there's plenty of pain on the way up.

That's not always true, of course. But it was true for me.

I chased an exit for millions because what gets rewarded gets repeated. The gratuitous exit is so graphically celebrated that I chased it to the exclusion of all else. I forsook the things most important to me to accomplish it. I turned my back on the people most important to me to get it.

"IPOs."

"Exits."

This is Business Porn talk.

And it will *destroy* your potential for the success that comes when you have a clear and compelling Owner's Intent.

Without it, I was nothing but a failure in Business Porn clothes.

Without a true Owner's Intent, every interesting idea that came along easily swayed me. I'd return from a conference inspired, ready to burn down everything we were already doing and start a whole bunch of new projects. Those new projects lasted just long enough for a whole new set of ideas to replace them, and then I eventually burned those down too.

Because I was a Business Porn-seeking, headless, flaming chicken.

My business coach tried to warn me one day over coffee.

"You have no idea what you want out of this company, so you're starting fires all the time," he said. "You're burning down projects, people, relationships, team members, customers. You're a visionary arsonist, and you don't know what you're trying to build or why you're trying to build it!"

That's a dangerous place to be.

If you don't know what you want out of your business, you'll be tempted to follow whatever is celebrated in your culture. The path of least resistance.

THE REAL COST OF DOING BUSINESS

I spoke to a business owner who recently sold his company for $5 billion, and now he feels utterly lost. He has a big, big pile of money and no purpose.

People hear his story and think, "Amazing! This guy started a company, grew it, and sold it for $5 billion. Now that's a sexy success story! That's what you're supposed to do."

Our culture drills porn-talk into us constantly. But what isn't on the front page of *Entrepreneur* magazine? That $5 billion cost him *everything* that mattered to him.

Because the "success" of that money was never his true, honest Owner's Intent. It was a mirage of what he wanted. Which means he *didn't* get what he wanted. And now maybe he never will. Since he lacked clarity, he chased the fantasy idea of success, got it, and now? He's empty. Business Porn will do that to you.

It's the opposite of Owner's Intent, which it turns out is what you need to be *happy*. Only you can answer what that is.

Please understand how conditioned you are to live someone

else's Intent. From childhood, you're conditioned with alien beliefs about what success is and isn't. But maybe someone else's winning is actually your version of failing. This definition of success has no relation to what you hold dear.

I had no idea that my business drive was coming from an unhealthy place. I thought I was just "good at business" and had a drive to be successful.

It's time to be real, raw, and honest again. You must be honest about where your drive comes from.

Do you know what's driving you? Do you know why you make the decisions you do?

I do now. The reality is, what was driving me was worse than anything I had imagined.

For thirty-six years, I'd been driven, all right.

I'd been driven by an inner demon.

THE AMERICAN NIGHTMARE

The Root Cause for Business Owner Stress and Anxiety

In 1987, I was a seven-year-old fiery redhead with a filthy mouth.

In fact, my nickname was Cussin' Casey. (My parents blamed my brother's friends for this.)

That year I was playing in the recreational basketball league. Let's just say I had a little bit of an anger problem, mostly due to a kid named Jason. Jason was on our rival team, and he made me so mad. I started getting fouls called because of my aggression on the court.

During one game, I vividly remember pushing Jason. I was benched the rest of the game.

After that miserable game, I received the first coaching session of my life. A fourteen-year-old gym sweeper named Ken delivered it.

His advice kept me from getting kicked out of the league.

From then on, seven-year-old Casey looked up to fourteen-year-old gym sweeper Ken.

At the time I didn't realize it, but Ken was doing way more than just sweeping floors. He was a hard worker and always knew how to make money. Even at fourteen, his no-B.S. attitude drew me in.

He was running the gym on the weekends with his brother, who handled the scoreboard.

And Ken was more than a floor sweeper.

- He was the star baseball player.
- He had a washboard belly, chiseled chin, and cool "Bama bangs" (that's what we called the frat-boy swoop bangs).
- He even made great grades.

Ken was Captain America of Pleasant Grove High School. Ken saved my rear in 1987. I was able to finish the season relatively unscathed.

Now let's fast-forward thirty years. I, the redheaded Cussin' Casey, had just sold a company for millions of dollars. Yet I was depressed.

From the outside, all those B.S. Business Porn hustlers said, "Wow, look at what you did, Casey. Congrats!" This made my depression worse. Obviously, I should have been happy. (Or so I thought.)

I'd accomplished a massive life goal: company sale. I could retire young with my beautiful wife and two kids. I was literally living the

American Dream. But I was sitting alone at a Starbucks, depressed, with dark thoughts I don't want to admit to having—as if I'd been fouled for aggressive behavior on the court.

This was so much worse. *It was my own personal American Nightmare.*

SELLING YOUR SOUL

How in the world, two weeks post-sale—when I had the bag of gold at the end of the rainbow—could this be hell?

Ask Judas (yes, *that* Judas).

Judas was among the A-team of Jesus's disciples. He said the right things, but his character was flawed. He sold Jesus out for thirty pieces of silver.

After the deed was done, there was no rainbow. He regretted his decision, left his blood money on the floor (since they wouldn't take it back), and hated himself to the point of self-destruction.

He hanged himself.

Not that I'm the backstabbing-apostle type or anything, but after selling my company, I get it.

I'd sold out my *people.*

My wretched million pieces of silver were meaningless because to sell my company, I hurt my most treasured relationships and made some very dumb decisions.

I failed at what *others* thought was success, and I had the scars to prove it.

I didn't like myself.

So after moping privately, I finally decided to meet with my friend Richard and proceeded to unload my feelings of guilt and discontent. "I don't even know why I exist," I said. "I think the world might be better off without me."

Here was the most painful one: "All I feel like I do is hurt people." My most prevailing thought was, *You got lucky. Now you're done. That was the best you'll ever experience.*

To my surprise, the money was meaningless because I hurt relationships to get it.

I looked at my bank account and thought, *Forget it all.*

Now I understood, at least in part, why Judas threw away his money. I didn't sell a company. I sold what propped me up as a human. My props had kept me distracted from myself and why I was so driven.

OUR TEAM

When you sell a company, you sell the team. I didn't realize how bad this would make me feel.

I'm not against selling a company, but you'd better know that when it's sold, the relationships change.

I was so driven for them to like me—now they didn't.

MEANINGFUL WORK

I sold my daily reason for getting out of bed excited.

In this Starbucks, two weeks after the sale and with nothing to do, I found out how important *meaningful work* is to me. I realized that I'll never retire. The lack of meaningful work, of making a difference in people's lives, is *hell* for me.

For the first time in my life, I experienced staring at the clock and just waiting until five to go home. Having a million in the bank and nothing to do that matters? It sucks. It sucked the life out of me, and it sucked the life out of those around me.

ACCOUNTABILITY

You know those office (or Zoom) meetings you hate to attend? I would have died to go to one.

Not having anywhere to be and having nobody counting on you may sound like a dream, but for me it was miserable. I'm at my best when I feel accountable to others.

Casey floating around with nothing to do, nowhere to be, and nobody counting on him leads to disaster, which is exactly what happened.

My relationships were unraveling. I had just sold my company, yet my wife and I were fighting for our marriage like never before.

We were distant, even alien, to each other. I had spent so many years pursuing external success that my most intimate relationship took the worst bruises. *I won at business but failed at home.*

I told Richard what was happening and my dark thoughts. I told him that my wife was telling me the truth about how I was, about what it truly was like to be on the other side of me.

I told him that I hated myself. I was failing as a husband and father. I was lonely. I was scared, yet everyone thought I should be happy.

SIDE NOTE

You might be thinking, *Poor Casey. If I had his money, I would be happy.* I get it. From the outside peering in, it's easy to think what made me miserable will make you happy. I promise you that you won't know for sure until you go on this journey to create your Owner's Intent. Suspend assumptions for just a little while longer.

JUDGMENT DAY

How in the world did this happen?

I didn't have an Owner's Intent. That's how. In fact, I had someone else's B.S., knockoff version I passed off as my own because I didn't know *what I really wanted.*

This time I wasn't about to get kicked out of a basketball league. This time I was on the brink of being kicked out of life by my own doings.

So I called my mentor and the now-head of our advisory board, Ken.

Yes, that Ken: Captain America of Pleasant Grove High School. Thirty years later, Ken is still one of the prime influencers in my life. When I met with Ken, he said two words that changed my life forever: "Call Joe."

"Who is Joe?" I replied.

"Joe is my coach," Ken replied, "and he's who you need."

I do whatever Ken tells me to do. Since I was seven years old, he's always kept me in the game.

I was on the phone with my mentor Joe that same day.

As mentioned earlier, we call Joe the Holy Spirit of Gravy. He has an uncanny ability to get you to open up and bare your soul. Instantly. I told Joe every dirty secret I had in our first forty-five minutes. I told him the stuff I thought I would take to my grave. I had no other option.

Joe listened. Then he said something that started an unforgettable, life-changing process. "You're normal," Joe said.

You see, Ken told me to call Joe because he regularly works with billionaire families. He confirmed that everything I told him was common, and the reason I felt so depressed was that I'd retired *from* something instead of *to* something.

"I want to meet with you," I said.

Not so fast. He made me do eight hours of soul-searching work before he would see me in person. This included going back and detailing every event in my life.

Stuff like:

- My first memory is having an earache and going to the emergency room when I was four years old.
- When I was thirteen, I drank my first beer at a Hootie and the Blowfish concert.
- I led the charge to set the senior bonfire on fire the night before the homecoming celebration.

It was a roundup of every memory. Big and small. Significant and insignificant.

After going through my life story for eight hours, when I finally met with Joe, he said something that rocked my soul: "Casey, the first thirty-six years have been all about you. You've been running from yourself, chasing success, and being liked. And at the end of the day, I feel like you are still trying to make your daddy proud of you."

(WTF?)

As I drove home, I just wept. Just like I'm doing as I am writing this. (Yes, those tears again.) Cognitively, I know my daddy loves me and is proud of me. Emotionally, I just want the phone to ring and hear him say it.

All my striving. All my pushing. All my aggression on the basketball court and my life comes down to me wanting to look in the stands and feel like he's proud.

WHO'S YOUR "DADDY"?

This chapter is a lot about me, but what about you? We all have these "daddy" moments. The question is: what's yours? Who's *your* daddy? Who or what is the thing that is secretly driving you?

I would have never known or admitted that I'd built and sold a company just to make my daddy proud, but that's what drives me. That's *who* drives me.

You are either running *from* something or *to* something. Cut the B.S. and ask yourself which it is. Can you get beneath the *seemingly* deep answers like:

- "I work so hard for my family."
- "I'm doing this to leave a legacy."
- "I'm trying to accomplish my goals."
- "I'm doing this for me."

Until you take the time to journal or get behind closed doors with a counselor to really uncover what or who is driving you, you will negatively affect yourself and the people around you for the rest of your life. The worst part? You likely don't even know it.

I called Ken after my sessions with Joe. "I finally know why I am the way I am," I told him with a slight smile. Even saying it released something in me.

I could start the process of thinking about what was next. My American Nightmare? Perhaps it actually could become the American Dream everyone thought it was.

Understanding what was driving me allowed me to start the process of being intentional about the next company I would start. Understanding who was driving me was the beginning of a true North Star.

It was the beginning of releasing what I thought I wanted and who I thought I was and a beginning of embracing the real, raw, and honest me, with my real, raw, and honest desires and drive.

I put down what others expected of me—and even what *I* expected of me—and instead picked up the authentic simplicity that exemplifies me. Both in business and in life.

And when I did, I found everything. I found my Owner's Intent.

YOU LYING S.O.B.

How Being Ruthlessly Honest with Yourself Can Skyrocket Your Business Growth

Owner: "Casey, I want a legacy business. One my kids own, for generational wealth."

Me: "Why does a legacy business matter to you?"

No answer.

Not a real one. She kept giving me answers that spoke to a different *why*:

- "Because we could go live in England for a few months at a time!"
- "We could *own* a home instead of renting."
- "We could pay someone to clean our house!"

She didn't want a legacy business. That was a way her brain told her she could have what she really wanted—to travel, buy a home, and hire someone else to clean it. She started with a lie to herself. She didn't mean to lie, but she lied nonetheless. Not only did she not want to have a generational business, she honestly didn't even know what that meant.

We have to stop lying about *why* we own businesses.

In creating your Owner's Intent, you will have to be *ruthlessly honest* about what you want this business to do for your life. You have to stop the B.S.

Remember the eight hours I spent getting ready for Joe?

I put this lady through the ringer.

After about six hours of working with this very smart woman, we got all her biggest dreams on paper. We discovered her business *already* made enough money to pay for what she really wanted, but we only discovered it once she got ruthlessly honest.

She wanted a certain kind of lifestyle. So we built her Owner's Intent to say, "I own this business to make $50,000 profit a month so I can fund my lifestyle."

This is an excellent Owner's Intent. It's specific, and most of all, it's ruthlessly honest.

Just think: the reason for the existence of a company *isn't always* what we say it is! She wasn't telling her customers, "This company exists to make me $50,000 a month!" She was telling them what they needed to hear to be her customers.

But under the hood, every decision came down to that monthly $50,000 profit. Now *that* creates a certain kind of company.

A company that exists so the owner can lift weights and pick up his kids from school is a radically different organization from the one that exists so the owner's kids can work there.

Notice that none of these Intents have anything to do with product, service, or branding.

But will these Intents *affect* the branding?

Hell yes. Hiring? Ditto. Spending? You get the picture. Everything about a company hinges on its reason for being, which is something deep inside the owner's head. Now she filters every business decision through the lens of her Owner's Intent.

Her pressure to grow is gone. She just needed to maintain her margins and take out the $50,000 monthly profit.

It's years later, and she is fulfilled as can be because she finally got raw, real, and ruthlessly honest about what she really wanted her business to do for her life.

What about you? What is on your list of what you want your business to give you?

RUTHLESSLY HONEST QUESTIONS TO ASK

- Do you want time freedom? How much do you want to work?
- Do you want to work with certain people? Name them.
- Do you want to make enough so your spouse can quit working? How much is that?
- Do you want to travel? How many trips do you want to take? What will they cost?

- Do you want to influence people? Which people? What does "influence" mean to you?
- Do you want to raise capital to scale because you want to create an IPO so you can be a public company CEO?
- Do you want to "change the world"? Which part of the world? How will you know when you've done it? Do you really want to change the *whole world*? Maybe you just want to change somebody's world?

FOOL'S GOLD

I want to rant on this last one.

Before you run off to be a hero, know that most people who *change the world* have terrible relationships. I won't name the household names, but if you want to live like them, you're going to give up *a lot* at home to change the world or save humanity.

And now you know the CEO secret: "changing the world" is probably just a cover for their hidden Owner's Intent. That earth-shaking company on the front page every day (and all the failed relationships in its wake) might just be the world's most elaborate plot to win a parent's love or prove self-worth. Inside, we're all about five years old.

So your Owner's Intent *must reflect* that.

If it doesn't, you're still lying to yourself, and no one is more guilty than me. Like my friend above, I, too, have lied to myself. I have not been *ruthlessly honest* about what I really want from my business.

I told myself, "I want to impact people!"

But in reality, I wanted to have no debt because my grandaddy killed himself from being overwhelmed from debt.

And really:

- I wanted to be a millionaire.
- I wanted to travel six to eight weeks a year.
- I wanted to be able to share experiences with my family and friends.

I lied when I told myself I wanted to impact people.

Impact? That's not Owner's Intent. Saying, "I want to make an impact," is like eating backyard barbeque ribs with a knife and fork instead of your hands. *Eat the meat like we know you want to!*

Who is your pretense fooling?

Only *you*.

We all do it. We all refuse to be real, raw, and ruthlessly honest. We all refuse to cut through our own B.S.

But if we stop lying to ourselves and instead dig deep to uncover what we *really* want, it will save us from hurting others. It will save us from hurting ourselves.

I told everyone in my last company that I cared about *impact*. But my actions were all about getting myself *rich*. Externally I shared that our purpose was to "empower church leaders," and while that did happen, the truth was that I cared more about being debt-free.

That's why I confused everyone when I sold my last company. They didn't know the deeper explanation of what I *really* wanted. They only knew the purpose I shared in public.

The only bad Owner's Intent is one that's *dishonest* or, in the case with my last company, *unclear*.

Let's revisit my friend Brian, the CEO from Dayton, Ohio, whom I met for hours in that coworking space. Brian coined the term "Owner's Intent." He was the person who helped me see that until I was ruthlessly honest, the business would never reach its full potential.

While I was talking about business outcomes that first meeting, Brian kept pushing back and pushing me forward to get to the root of "why I own Gravy."

Two months and lots of soul searching later, I ended up with mine. Do you remember? If not, here it is again:

> *To build a company my adult kids would want*
> *to work at someday if they so choose.*

This is a real Intent. This is what drives me daily.

Because I was able to release the drive for my dad's approval, I'm now free to chase a vision that is in line with what I *really* want from my business.

I am free to run *to* something I really need rather than *from* something I don't really want.

This is hard to do alone. It's easy to lie to yourself, just like I did.

So I created audio content and a worksheet at dontfail.biz/intent to help coach and guide you to get closer to your Intent than ever before.

Because if you are truly committed to winning when others fail, here is a prime way others fail. They refuse to stop lying to themselves.

You can be different. (Plus, you committed at the beginning of the book to not lie, right?)

Start becoming honest—ruthlessly honest—with yourself to uncover your *real* Intent for your business.

Your Owner's Intent.

JUDGMENT DAY

How to Mute External Voices "Shoulding" All Over Your Business

The same year I was getting in trouble on the basketball court, I also went to a church event called Vacation Bible School (VBS).

I went because it was basically free childcare for my parents. I liked going because of the red Kool-Aid from the orange pitchers.

After making plaster-of-paris praying hands, we went into the sanctuary of the old Baptist church. I remember it like it was yesterday. The preacher said something like this:

> *"When you die, you will sit outside the gates of heaven, and they will play a movie of all the bad things you have done. The Lord sits on the judgment seat and will not allow you to come in unless you confess that Jesus Christ is your Lord! If you don't do this, you will burn in hell."*

So Cussin' Casey was sitting there, pondering this at seven.

Let me get this straight, I thought, *if I walk down the aisle and talk to the preacher, I don't have to watch the bad movie of myself and go to hell?*

It didn't take long for me to have my answer. Half a second, actually. *Ummm, I'm in!* I got baptized that Sunday to ensure my ticket into heaven. Of course, looking back, I see how my VBS experience was a joke.

Still, my fear of judgment was no laughing matter.

Most owners fail because they don't become real, raw, and brutally honest about *why* they own a business. They fail because of fear. Specifically, their *fear of judgment.*

The judgment from family, friends, team members, other business owners—and themselves.

We feel like we *should* build the business a certain way because of what people will think of us.

Owner's Intent saves you from judgment (yes, that was a bad pun). Getting clear on your Owner's Intent holds the same weight as getting clear on getting rid of the fear of judgment in your life.

CUT TO THE CHASE

I met a guy one time who had a really awesome knife-making business. The price for one knife *started* at $10,000.

You can imagine he had a lot of demand. In fact, he was so behind in his orders that there was a nine-month waiting list.

Being Mr. "Let's Offer Some Business Advice When He Didn't Ask" Casey, I said, "If it takes that long to produce, you're delaying payments and income. Why don't you hire one person as an apprentice and double your production speed without losing your quality? Then you can actually take orders faster, make more money, and do half the work!"

A stroke of brilliance.

SIDE NOTE

One of my mentors' names was Regi. He died the year I wrote this book. He told me, "Unasked-for advice is always taken as judgment." I wish he'd told me this five years earlier when I was dishing out advice to the knife maker.

The bladesmith looked at me and said, "Because I want to make the knives. I don't want to do that." He went on to tell me that he had decided to keep his business all to himself and explained the unique value that accrued to himself, his family, and the market because of his decisions.

One happy knife maker taught me not to judge another man's Owner's Intent.

NO WRONG WAY TO BE RIGHT

Remember, there is no wrong Owner's Intent—if you're honest. If you cut through the B.S.

The only way to be wrong is to knowingly—or more likely, *unknowingly*—lie to yourself and others about why you own the business.

I met a woman who grew a business and sold it the month before she had her first baby.

She said, "My goal was to grow a business large enough to sell before I became a mom so I can just be a mom and have the financial benefit of selling the company."

Now that is a *fantastic* Owner's Intent. It's clear, time-specific, and honest.

One of my mentors' Owner's Intent is to grow his software company to a $1 billion valuation and go public.

Again, another excellent Owner's Intent—assuming this is his *truest* intent.

I have a buddy who owns a surfing business. His self-proclaimed Owner's Intent is to live in "Bob Marley Mode," which he said means, "I want to play golf two times a week and be free to be with my kids whenever I want."

I absolutely love this Intent.

Your Intent will inform everything else.

- The happy knife maker won't hire.
- The mom won't feel guilty.

▪ The surfer won't do things to restrict his freedom.

But if they didn't have these nailed down, Business Porn would get the best of them, and they'd constantly live in angst about what they "should" be doing—or not doing.

You will command more respect from your market, your team, your family, your friends, and yourself when you honestly and clearly proclaim *why* you do what you do.

People might judge. But that's on them, not you. In fact, they might have to sit and watch that damn bad movie of themselves at the pearly gates.

But you? You'll be living free thanks to your Purpose, *on purpose*, while they're wading knee-deep in the B.S. "shoulds" instead of what they really want. Instead of living from their Owner's Intent.

Like you'll be.

WHAT IF I'M WRONG?

Making this Commitment Ensures Fulfillment and Success

Right before I walked through the church doors to get married, one of my groomsmen asked me, "Are you sure she's the one?"

Not cool. I was like, "What the heck?"

If you've ever made the decision to get formally engaged, you've experienced the head trash around *committing*. Head trash is about fear of commitment—fear of being wrong and stuck.

My groomsman was clearly head trash personified.

This fear is why commitment is supposed to be serious. Once you put a ring on it (cue Beyoncé) or set the wedding date, you'll be scorned for changing it. You'll be scorned since we all assumed you knew what you were getting yourself into and made a lot of big life decisions around it, like joint bank accounts and matching toothbrushes.

Business owners know what I'm talking about.

The number one reason business owners do not get radically clear on their Owner's Intent is that they have commitment issues.

And the reason for commitment issues is thinking they can't *change* their Intent.

Here's some good news: you absolutely can.

Your Owner's Intent is yours. It's not objective reality. Are you going to change? Yes. Is your life going to change? Yes!

By now, you can probably rattle off my *current* Owner's Intent:

> *To create a company my adult kids would want*
> *to work at one day if they so choose.*

I chose this because it reflects what I know *now*. But if I get a call from my wife that she has cancer, do you think that will change?

Absolutely.

I don't know the exact phrasing, but it would become something like: "To have enough stable cash flow to pay for the medical bills and be fully present for her whenever she needs me."

That's extreme, but it's real, raw, and honest. Your Owner's Intent serves you and those around you *right now*.

NO DOUBT

I'd say this makes your Owner's Intent on a far lesser order of magnitude than saying "I do" to your spouse. The problem with a lot of business owners is they treat their commitment to a spouse lower than their commitment to their business.

When I started Gravy, I put a seven-year horizon on my commitment to the company. As we are now only four years into that vision, I expect to extend that horizon.

People are always waiting for the right time to start or invest because of fear of commitment.

However, the right time to decide is *right now*. Your decision to *decide* is the one choice that makes all of your next decisions easy. This decision is at stake every moment you don't make it.

You have an interrupting groomsman in your brain saying, "Are you sure? Really sure? How about now—can you really be sure *now*?"

Notice that the groomsman doesn't offer you any evidence you're wrong. He just offers doubt on a platter.

That's all he's got. You're putting off making the best decisions because of doubt. And it's all a fake-out. There's no way to answer the questions doubt raises because you're not the person who will answer them—*yet*. You won't be until you make the decision.

Beyond doubt, there's certainty. What can you know for certain? You can have your *values* in place. Namely:

- What value do you put on your relationships?
- What value do you put on your business?

Start to know yourself. Then you can begin to figure out your Owner's Intent from a place of present certainty rather than future doubt.

STICKY STATEMENTS

The One-Sentence Decision-Making Filter for You and Your Team

Let's talk politics!

In 2007, Barack Obama was relatively unknown by most people in the United States. In 2008, he was the forty-fourth president of the United States.

There are many reasons he won, but one of the absolutely obvious reasons was because of his one-word message: change.

John McCain was his competitor. I've asked one hundred-plus people what his message was, and nobody knows. Why? Because it wasn't good. (It was "Country first.")

What about Donald Trump? He might be the most unlikely winner ever in the U.S. presidential race. When he was running, some thought it was a publicity stunt. However, he won.

Again, there are many reasons, but one of them was his slogan: "Make America great again."

His opponent, Hillary Clinton had three different slogans and messages during her run against Trump. Can you remember them? Or even one of them? Probably not. None of them stuck.

Obama and Trump created *statements that stick*. When you do this, you win, your team wins, and everyone around you wins.

Why? The answer lies in Alpharetta, Georgia.

GETTING STICKY WITH IT

My pastor's name is Andy Stanley. He leads a network of churches in the Atlanta area, with the main campus located in the suburban city of Alpharetta.

SIDE NOTE

Want to learn how to communicate? Speak publicly? Structure a presentation? Watch Andy on TV or online. Seriously, I know this is a business book, but he is the single best communicator I know. And communication is vital to your success in business.

He said something that has helped me communicate to everyone around me. He says, "Memorable is portable," which means that if you can't *remember* it, you can't *repeat* it.

When I ask owners to tell me exactly why they own their business, in one sentence, they can't. They ramble. Like I did when Brian asked me mine in our first meeting in Dayton, Ohio.

You've had a little bit of time to start thinking about it. So let's put it to the test. Right now, stop reading, and tell me your Owner's Intent if you think you've got it. Answer this question in *one clear sentence:* why do you own your company? *For real.* Do it! Start talking.

Still can't, huh? You aren't alone. It's hard.

Even though mine took sixty days of hashing out, yours can take a lot less because you can learn from my failures and get to the heart of your Intent.

CLEAR AS DAY

There are three reasons your Owner's Intent must be crystal clear.

1. CERTAINTY FOR YOU

This is important as a solid Owner's Intent becomes your rock of certainty and makes you more successful. It will give you confidence when the world beats the hell out of you and your business. Because there is power in saying, "This is it. This is why I own this business."

It also filters out doubt when you need to make tough calls on personnel and serves as the single statement that guides your money decisions.

You will be more successful with the clarity of your why.

2. CLARITY FOR YOUR TEAM

So many frustrations are due to a team's inability to read the owner's mind. In fact, as owners, we often tell people they should "think like an owner."

Well, that's not true. Maybe *an* owner, but not *the* owner.

They should each think with their personal Owner's Intent. But you can only be responsible for your own.

Plus, they have their own perceptions of what you, as *the* owner, should or shouldn't do. Just like all constituents do.

Since your Owner's Intent is your responsibility, it's on *you* to communicate it. Tell them your Owner's Intent all the time. In fact, when you think you have told them too much, you are just getting started.

It *needs* to stick.

So tell them before you hire them, during training, and as long as they stay on your team.

Otherwise, they won't take it seriously, and you'll degrade their trust. They'll be saying, even mentally, *Hey, what happened to that slogan she was saying? Oh, I get it. This is just another place with empty words.*

Why the owner *owns* the business matters—it's part of your company's internal communications. This helps your team members, contractors, and even vendors know how your organization fits their personal career path.

3. CONFIDENCE FOR EVERYONE

If you want everyone to be more confident in you, speak clearly and confidently about why you own your business. You'll win over your investors, spouse, partner, and friends—and most of all, yourself.

HOW TO MAKE STICKY STATEMENTS

What would a sticky statement look like for your Owner's Intent?

"I want to have $1 million in personal cash in three years."

That's right: *personal cash*. Every person should know this, and it will guide and govern everything you all do.

I know what you're thinking. *Casey, I'm going to tell people that I'm in it for $3 million bucks?*

Of course you are. You *have to*. Because $3 million is your *why*. In fact, you can expect everyone to have a why and spill it—at least to you privately. If you're honest about how they're helping you get to $3 million, you'll also allow *them* to be honest about what they want from *you*.

Get everyone to talk about *what's in it for them*. Radical transparency will allow you to explain how you'll help them to reach their dreams, just like they're helping you to reach yours.

Here are some examples of a *clear* Owner's Intent:

"I want to have the flexibility to homeschool my kids."

This clear intent helps anyone you hire know *without a doubt* you will not be working all day. Also, they know your kids' education is more important than the business's needs. They will hope, if not expect, that you'll afford them the same or similar treatment— because that's the kind of company you're building. You will draw the right team members who value what you value.

> *"I want to create an IPO and become CEO*
> *of a publicly traded company."*

Well, now you know you probably are going to need to raise money. It informs your path. You're also going to attract team members who want this trajectory and repel team members who value flexibility.

> *"I want to create a company that my adult*
> *children will want to work for."*

For me, this says a few things. Namely how we treat people at Gravy, my current company, is the top priority—culture above all. We also must be strong enough to last because my kids are young! Lastly, we have great benefits and support people when they leave. Why? You guessed it: because I want *my* kids supported.

Look, people fail miserably at a lot. Myself included. But if you want to be truly successful, you have to do the work to build this right. *Right now.* Right before the B.S. hacks start to creep back in.

Let's build your Owner's Intent.

MY BOUDOIR PHOTOGRAPHY SESSION

The Step-By-Step Guide to Crafting the Most Important Sentence of Your Career

Three big drivers determine why people own businesses.

1. Income (money)
2. Independence (time)
3. Influence (impact)

Most owners have one or two of these that primarily drive why they own their own company. But things can get tricky when we try to identify them.

Meet my boudoir photographer (no, it's not what you think. I'm far from her ideal client). If you're not sure what a boudoir photographer is, let's just say it's beyond the scope of this book.

She said her Owner's Intent was "to unleash the power of women."

However, every time I coached her, all she spoke about was building a $100-million company.

Even crazier is how she frantically texted me when sales were bad or a launch didn't go well. She wasn't stressed about making women look good. She stressed about making good money. I called her on it. Because you know *what drives you the most by what stresses you out the most.*

Read that again.

She thought her driver was Influence. In reality, it was really Income.

So I propose you dig down into these three areas: Income, Independence, and Influence. If you follow my steps below, you will cut through the B.S. hacks and develop a solid Owner's Intent that will guide your business and life.

THE RULES FOR CREATING YOUR OWNER'S INTENT

1. **It must be one sentence.** Two is good, but try for one.
2. **It must be yours.** Don't use mine. Don't borrow anyone else's. Don't let anyone else "should" on you. Remember that it can be as unique as you.
3. **It must be pressure-tested.** When will it fail a stress test? You must think through future business and personal situations and put it under pressure to see if it stands the weight of reality. I'll help you do that in this chapter.

AVOID THESE AT ALL COSTS

While those are the things you *must* do, there are also five things you must avoid like the plague when creating your Owner's Intent.

1. AVOID THINKING YOU "SHOULD" HAVE A PARTICULAR INTENT.

You'll think you know the real answer faster than you do. You don't yet. It takes real time and thought to find out your *deepest* drivers. (You know how I told you I prepared for that one meeting with my mentor Joe for eight hours? Do that.)

2. AVOID WHAT *OTHERS* THINK YOU "SHOULD" DO.

Your uncle who thinks the government is out to get you shouldn't sway your opinion of why *you* own your company and make the decisions you make. (Nor should your parents, who you are probably trying to make happy on some level.)

Don't even let your significant other try to sway your Intent. You have to get down to *you* being 100 percent real, raw, and honest with *yourself*.

3. AVOID WHAT YOU THINK YOU *CAN* OR *CAN'T* DO.

For example, your Owner's Intent might be "to exit for $10 million cash." You might not know *how* that will happen, but it doesn't matter for your Intent. Don't limit yourself to what you know now. First and foremost is knowing who you are.

4. AVOID WHAT ANYONE *ELSE* THINKS YOU CAN OR CAN'T DO.

Don't let your broke stepdad (and especially your rich uncle) tell you what you can't accomplish. Don't let losers and people who just sit and watch the news all day tell you what your future can or cannot be. Don't let the successful or judgmental shame you either. When it happens, admit you feel ashamed, and move on. Just face the feeling and move past it to find the real you.

5. AVOID WHAT *SOUNDS* GOOD OR NOBLE.

Your Owner's Intent doesn't have to be a cause-driven why. I disagree with popular author and speaker Simon Sinek on this. I think it can be whatever you want it to be as long as it's honest and keeps you out of jail.

If you choose "My Intent is to have enough cash to buy exotic cars so I can effortlessly get a date," that's fine by me. At least you're honest. Somebody else reading this will get mad about that. He'll judge you, but you shouldn't care. Why? *You will do it anyway.*

You will have a nice car, order manhattans at the swanky bar, and hope to get a date like you saw a guy do last time you were in Vegas.

You will always act on your Intent because that's already what you do. So just say it.

A business, and success in business, allows you to act on your primal Intent at more effective levels than you've ever known.

That's why CEOs are not, by definition, the world's arbiters of high moral standards. More so, they've shown the discipline to create a system for just getting more of what they want.

STEP BY STEP

The first step of getting your Owner's Intent out of your head is to get it onto paper. So I recommend writing it rather than saying it.

Whether you think your driver is Income, Independence, or Influence, we will break down all three with a helpful exercise to get to the root of each driver.

These questions are important. Spend some time answering each.

DRIVER 1: INCOME

Questions to answer: What is the primary financial outcome you want from your business? When do you want it?

Tell me the first answer you can think of: _____

Next, let's pressure test it and discover your real intent. We'll use the "five whys" exercise I learned from a coach named Rob.

Exercise: Your Five Whys

What are your whys? Yes, plural. Because when you want to get to the heart of something, you have to ask why five times. You can't rush this. Don't waste your life on weak answers for the sake of speed.

That's why my life sucked in the first companies I owned. I was too fast to pressure test my why. I was too driven. (Or not driven enough. This takes a *deeper level of drive*.)

Here's how to dig down to your real Intent.

Let's say you begin with the Owner's Intent:

Why #1: Why do you want this business?

"I want to have $1 million in cash in the next three years."
Great! Now write down the answers to the following questions:

Why #2: Why is $1 million in cash important to me?

"I've always wanted to be a millionaire."
Great! Ask again:

Why #3: Why is being a millionaire important to me?

"Because I want financial certainty."
And what lies beneath *that?*

Why #4: Why is financial security important to me?

"Because I don't want financial stress like I had in my house growing up."
Interesting.

Why #5: Why is avoiding my childhood financial stress important to me?

"Because my parents got a divorce."
Bingo.

So the real, raw, and honest reason you want $1 million in cash in the next three years isn't the million, nor is it to be a millionaire.

No, your Owner's Intent is really "to have $1 million in three years to protect my marriage from financial stress."

Let me ask you a question. If you joined a business and the owner told you this story—that it's all for the sake of a solid marriage—how much more respect would you have for your boss?

This is an example of the power of the real why. Your raw, real, honest *why* is attractive, both to yourself and others. It will be the flux capacitor for your business fulfillment and success.

(I love Doc Brown from *Back to the Future*. On some days, I feel like him: a lunatic mad scientist making up stuff, hoping it will work.)

DRIVER 2: INDEPENDENCE

Question to answer: what do you want to be able to decide about your time/schedule?

Tell me the first answer you can think of: _____

This is super important. *It's complete B.S. to act like a victim of your business schedule.* You don't miss your kid's performances, conferences, games, and appointments because of your business. You miss them because your child isn't part of your Intent. It's that simple.

Get your scheduling priorities straight:

- Do you want to live in Bob Marley Chill Mode?
- Do you want to work (or not work) on weekdays?

- Do you dream of heading to the pool and sipping on hard lemonade while passive income hits your account?
- Do you want to travel for work? How much?

As for me, I love having a forty-hour-a-week, full-time job, with six weeks off a year.

Three of those weeks are true vacation. The other three weeks are me kind of working from another location, like the British Virgin Islands. That's what *I* want.

I want to work most of the time because it's best for my emotional and mental health to be committed to a Mission and to a group of people beyond me. Again, that's what *I* want.

But for you, it might be to work four hours a week with passive income so you can tour with your band.

Same rules apply for this driver. You must pressure test it with the five whys on paper.

You may realize your Owner's Intent is purely driven by *schedule*:

*"To build a company that allows
me to get my kids off the bus every day and
volunteer in their classroom."*

Or:

*"To work eight hours a week and have
$2,000 per month passive income."*

These are powerful because if time is your driver and the business is taking all your time, you will live a mad and frustrated life.

DRIVER 3: INFLUENCE

Question to answer: What kind of impact do you want to have from owning your business?

Tell me the first answer you can think of: _____

People's thoughts and feelings about influence are wildly varied. Some people say, "I don't care about influence." That's fine. Your time or money might be the dominant factors.

On the other hand, your Intent might be "to create enough income to fund thirty schools in Kenya over the next five years." That's a darn good Intent. People will love to stand with you for that.

It could also be "to help military spouses have meaningful work."

Whatever you think you want to do, pressure test it with the five whys.

SAVE YOURSELF

After you've asked yourself the five whys regarding Income, Independence, and Influence, there are four more questions to ask about what you've discovered. Here's a handy acronym.

Answering these questions will SAVE you:

1. **Sacrifice**: What am I willing to give up to achieve my Owner's Intent? What am I *not* willing to give up?

2. **Agreement**: Do the people with whom I'm closest whole-heartedly agree with my Owner's Intent? Why or why not?
3. **Violation**: If my Owner's Intent is violated, what level of stress will it cause in my life? Why?
4. **Execution**: Do I want to execute every decision based on my Owner's Intent? This includes decisions about money, people, time, processes, and action.

Want to learn even more about your Owner's Intent? We have an entire website and guide at dontfail.biz/intent.

You can also visit dontfail.biz/intent to send me your Owner's Intent.

I hope I've demonstrated that discovering your Owner's Intent is the most important thing you do in your business, even though it's less about business and more about you.

Your Owner's Intent will now drive your Business Intent. Build it, and success and freedom will come. Own it, and you will be further along in designing a winning business and life.

Most business owners fail before they even begin by not doing the dirty work of cutting through their own crap to get at the heart of what they really want.

Which will you choose?

PART 2

NO-B.S. BUSINESS STRATEGY

"Clarity of vision

creates clarity of priorities."

—John C. Maxwell

Vision. Mission. Purpose. Values.

What comes to mind when you think of these terms? Are they bloated with empty words and promises to yourself and your business? Are they mere jargon and corporatese?

Or do they drip with integrity and authenticity?

If your real, raw, and honest answer is their Purpose serves no purpose, then it's time to think again.

In this part, you will learn how to take action to create a Mission, Vision, Purpose, and Core Values that are living, breathing, and accurate reflections of the business you really want and the actions you expect those around you to take to get there.

This part is more than empty words and pithy statements; it's about structuring a *culture of care* so you can recruit and hire employees who care and coach up or (you guessed it) fire those who don't.

SIAMESE DREAMS

How to Structure Your Business for Ultimate Satisfaction

Smashing Pumpkins released an album in 1993 called *Siamese Dream*. It was their breakthrough record. I would sit in my bedroom wearing Teva sandals, with a Banana Republic T-shirt tucked into my Umbros, teaching myself each track from *Siamese Dream* on my guitar.

I think every band that has "made it" has a story of not following the gurus, the hacks. Music is one of those industries where it's basically impossible to B.S. your way to the top. It requires a lot of failing on the way to creating music that resonates with a popular audience.

However, it also requires a ton of clarity as they go. There are far too many distractions on the way to the top, much less *at the top*.

(Does that sound like any entrepreneurs you know?)

So when thinking about structuring your business, you must first gain *massive clarity on your role within the business*. Specifically, how you can coexist with the operator of your business as you move from running your business to truly owning it.

But in order to do that, we first must get clear on how to reconcile the roles and how to manage the tension that exists.

SIAMESE TWINS: THE DUAL DISASTER

To put it simply, every founder is one person with two heads. They both *own* and *operate* the business. *Owners* create a crystal-clear Owner's Intent; *operators* give the owner what they want to be satisfied.

When the owner and operator are separate people, this conflict is much easier to manage. However, when these roles reside within the same person—as they likely do with you—the owner can be a recipe for disaster. As one human with two heads, it's hard to separate the two and see yourself in this dual role.

In these cases, you have to see yourself for who you really are: an *owner-operator*. It's not merely an external CEO versus COO; it's your internal owner versus your internal operator. When you don't gain massive clarity and create structure to separate the two roles inside you, you'll always be at war.

The victor? More often than not, it will be your operator. This will make the owner inside you miserable because there will constantly be an internal battle of unresolved tension.

Owner You versus Operator You

Owners think about:	Operators think about:
• Leadership	• Doership
• Possibility	• Reality
• Strategy	• Structure
• People	• Income
• Influence	• Execution
• Empowerment	• Compensation
• Culture	

As you see, your *Siamese Dream* quickly becomes a *Siamese Nightmare*. Learn how to avoid this mess by way of reading the warning signs and making pivots when necessary to move into the driver's seat by establishing massive clarity as the owner.

THE FIRST WARNING: UNCLEAR OWNERS PRODUCE WASTEFUL OPERATORS

Owner's Intent matters to operators. When the Intent isn't clear, operators waste time, money, and energy. This is true whether you're an owner-operator or an owner who hired a COO.

- **Wasted time:** The unclear operator doesn't invest time wisely.
- **Wasted money:** If the owner is unclear, they squander money on activities that will not make them happy.
- **Wasted energy:** This also might be one of the costliest because the owner has limited energy to lift the business where they want it to go without 100 percent focus.

THE SECOND WARNING: UNSATISFIED OWNERS PRODUCE UNMOTIVATED OPERATORS

If you aren't clear, the operator will not deliver. When the operator doesn't give the owner what they want, the owner feels angry, and the operator gets ornery. It's a case of bad communication, which creates a pattern of pain and distrust. It's a crazy cycle, but one that can end with massive clarity.

SIDE NOTE

If you haven't yet arrived at your Owner's Intent, go back to Part 1 and do it. I know. I hate rules and said you can read out of order. But to get the most out of this part, I recommend you at least nail your Owner's Intent. Really. Go do it now.

Part 2 hinges on you having that clear because I'm about to explain how to build your business as an operator, or for when you hire an operator.

TAKING CARE OF BUSINESS

Every Friday at 9:00 a.m., schedule an owner's meeting, which requires serious prep because of this meeting's importance.

In fact, you can even dress the part quite literally, especially if you need the visual if you are meeting with "operator you." Visit dontfail.biz, where you'll find a real hat with the word "Owner" on it. Do yourself a favor and grab one.

Okay, you have your hat on, and let's say it's next Friday: Owner's Meeting Day. Today is the day you'll meet with the operator of your business, regardless if it's you or an external COO.

In this meeting, you will:

- Define how the **Five Ps** relate to your Owner's Intent:
  - Your **personal** involvement in the company.
  - The **people** investments you make or don't make.
  - The **process** improvements you undertake.
  - Your **product** innovation schedule.
  - The **profitability** of your business.
- Develop a **strategy** to help your COO create your processes.

Now that you have massive clarity on how to help the owner and operator coexist as you move into your owner seat much more effectively, let's get *massively clear* on how to structure your business for your ultimate satisfaction as the owner.

I CAN SEE CLEARLY NOW

The Case for Vision Clarity

In order to structure your business for your Owner's Intent, your operator has to establish Vision Clarity. You cannot have one without the other.

You have to make sure that your Vision is not only clear and compelling but that it is owned by everyone on the team. Vision Clarity is a hallmark concept that will move you closer to being clear from the top to the bottom of your organization.

This is a big deal. It's one thing for you to know your business as the owner; it's another for those around you to know it. This simple test will help structure your team members' alignment around your Vision.

Here is the bottom line: the owner has to be clear about the Intent, but the operator must be clear about Vision Clarity. In fact, Vision Clarity is the operator's job. (Notice we're in the strategy section, but really, we're talking about Vision and clarity? It's no accident.)

A word of no-B.S. warning: until this becomes clear for all involved, you will not have the business of your dreams.

THE WHITE PAPER TEST

In order to lead out of Vision Clarity—which is where you ultimately want to be—you have to establish a baseline of where everyone is and what everyone thinks as it relates to your business's Purpose, Mission, and Values.

We do this simple test with our team a few times a year to get us all back on the same page.

THE GROUND RULES

- You can't ask anyone else for their answers.
- You must answer each question within sixty seconds (so a three-minute time limit).
- No shaming or penalties for wrong answers. You want to know what people really think.

THE TEST

Have each person on your team pull out a piece of paper.

Answer these three questions in the time allotted:

- What's the *Purpose* of your business? Why do you exist?

- What's the current *Mission* of your business? What's most important right now?
- What are the *Values* of your business?

If you have ten people, I guarantee you will have ten different answers. This test is a great way to recalibrate your team and get everyone back in alignment. It's the best way we've found to cut through the fluff and get the clarity owners need to structure for Intent. And you cannot do that without clarity surrounding your vision.

Let's break down the pieces of Vision Clarity.

VISION CLARITY

PURPOSE

Why does this business exist?

For Gravy, the company's Purpose is "We Accelerate Freedom." Seems vague, right? That's on purpose. Your Purpose needs to be the deeper why.

Let's dig deeper:

- **We** = A team. (It doesn't say "I.")
- **Accelerate** = Speed up.
- **Freedom** = The life options of our clients, partners, and teams.

Example:

We had a client email us and say, "My goal for the money you save us is to hire my husband full-time so he can work with me in my business. He hates his job, and I need the help."

Six months later we got another email: "My husband quit his job today because of the money you saved us. We hired him, and it's our dream come true!"

Without Gravy, this professional couple would have waited much longer than six months. We *accelerated* her husband's *freedom* from a terrible job. We accelerated her freedom of time because she was overwhelmed.

You might be thinking, *Why does this matter?*

I'd say, "You're missing the whole point."

"We Accelerate Freedom" is the battle cry of the operator to clients, partners, and team members. It's the rally point because it's what we *all* care about.

After you hear about how we changed someone's life thanks to the company Vision, if you're not fired up about it, we're not going to hire you. Or you're likely not going to stick around.

MISSION

What's your current Mission?

Like I said, if you ask ten people, you will get ten different answers. I've even found that when I ask solopreneurs, they give about five answers.

The current Mission is the *focus* of the business for now. In the business world, there's so much hollow advice and fluff out there that it's easy to get off track and get stuck, which is why the B.S. hacks are so attractive.

But when you are laser focused on the Mission at hand, you'll begin to see what's Mission critical—and what's not.

Gravy's current Mission is "to return $1 billion back to businesses by 2023."

Every operational decision of time and money is focused on this. Until we reach $1 billion returned, our current product stays focused on this *one* thing. It cuts out any confusion of what matters. It aligns the team to a macro focus.

Nothing has protected Gravy more than this. There are so many opportunities and ideas, and the question we all come back to is "How does this help us return $1 billion back to businesses?"

It's the filter for strategy and operations, and it's a good way to explain why you can't work on every person's great idea. It also keeps our friend the visionary arsonist (remember him?) in check.

VALUES

What are your Values?

The answers to this question are always a disaster when we do the White Paper Test in other companies. People are all over the place.

As the operator, Values matter because they define:

- How we treat people around here.
- What we allow.
- What we don't allow.

It's a behavior framework that creates the culture of the company. Owners often spend so much time frustrated because people don't do their jobs how the owner believes they should.

I'll tell you why.

Because 90 percent of the time, the Owner has never clarified their Values to clearly communicate how they want their team to act and treat others. Values clarify the rules.

Here is the chart of Gravy's five Core Values, plus what they *do* mean and *don't* mean.

We Build Others Up	
DOES MEAN	**DOESN'T MEAN**
Appreciating others specifically.	Withholding praise of others.
Unlocking potential through belief in others.	Allowing current circumstances and results to dictate and determine our trajectory.
Confronting with care.	Diminishing others and relationships through gossip.
Valuing people as humans.	Treating people like objects.

We Do What We Say We'll Do

DOES MEAN	DOESN'T MEAN
Valuing progress over perfection.	Letting perfection get in the way of necessity.
Leading with yes and knowing our limits.	People-pleasing that drives overcommitment.
Taking internal responsibility regardless of external circumstances.	Allowing external factors to become excuses.
Providing needed clarity and seeking continued clarity.	Giving or accepting ambiguous expectations.

We Don't Take Ourselves Too Seriously

DOES MEAN	DOESN'T MEAN
Being light, loose, and approachable.	Being rigid, close-minded, and hurried.
Having a heart of work hard and play hard.	Allowing your work to define your value.
Learning from failure creates strength.	Believing failure means weakness.
Realizing accomplishments are only as good as those they benefit.	Using accomplishments to create security.
Having agility and ability to move quickly.	Being unwilling, conscious or unconscious, to let go.

We Take Initiative

DOES MEAN	DOESN'T MEAN
Seeing the opportunity.	Waiting to be told what to do.
Growing persistently.	Settling for status quo.
Starting with self leadership.	Believing growth is automatic.
Identifying and creating solutions.	Stopping at pointing out problems.

We Approach Life with Optimism

DOES MEAN	DOESN'T MEAN
Resolving that we will win in the end.	Putting limits on our possibilities.
Confronting the brutal facts of our current reality.	Keeping bad news to ourselves.
Believing the best in others.	Assuming we know all the facts.
Bringing a positive presence.	Allowing circumstances to define our attitude.

If you aren't clear on Values, you will never build a business that satisfies the owner. It's like a slot machine reel, and you need to get three in a row to win:

1. When you clarify the Vision, you can motivate your team's heart with it.
2. When you clarify the Mission, you can lead your team with confidence toward a clear outcome.
3. When you clarify Values, you can lead your team to act the way you want.

I guarantee this is another area most business gurus will skip past in the race to feed you B.S. hacks. But this is the most important stuff for winning where others fail.

I spend 80 percent of my time pulling levers to win on all three. For the rest of the book, I'll show you exactly what that means and how to lead with Vision Clarity.

Don't miss this.

THE VACCINE FOR EMPLOYEES NOT GIVING A SH*T

Something that will keep your business from winning is being ping-ponged between too many opinions. There are too many ideas, opinions, and strategies. Better to go deep into just a few minds than bounce between them all.

Mastery is made from less, not more:

- *One* Owner's Intent
- *One* Vision
- *One* Purpose
- *One* Mission

Having *one* good relationship is much harder than dating several. It's also much more effective to reach your goal and make you an owner who lives happily ever after.

If you are going to be a solopreneur and have nobody work with you, you can skip this chapter. However, if you are going to build a business that involves hiring other people, this chapter is a must.

Vision Clarity aligns the Owner's Intent with the team. Your Purpose is the first part of Vision Clarity.

There are nine thousand opinions about how to develop your Vision and Purpose in your business. I struggled like hell. I failed. I made it really, really complicated for a long time.

Your business's Purpose is basically the deeper reason the business exists. This is super important to develop and share. It's the heartbeat of your business.

GRAVY'S PURPOSE: WE ACCELERATE FREEDOM

We Accelerate Freedom for our team members:

Jamie, our teammate, worked in a little business in a small town in Alabama.

They might have had a cow pie competition there, too, but Jamie wasn't betting money on poop like I did. Jamie earned a 29 (out of 36!) on her ACT and has amazing interpersonal skills.

However, Jamie worked in a closet at a local business and had no upward potential. Maybe she would get an annual raise. But she wasn't on any course of massive personal growth.

Jamie saw a friend post about her company taking all staff to Cancún for one of their company summits and became interested. That company is Gravy.

Jamie started in an entry-level position and dominated it for a year. She worked on developing her leadership, and she was recently promoted. Now she is running a team and a book of business worth millions of dollars.

(Talk about improvement over the closet.)

Gravy was able to act on its Purpose and *accelerate freedom* for Jamie.

- She has more financial freedom.
- She has more career freedom (she gets recruited all the time, and that's fine with me!).
- She has freedom of choices now, which she didn't have last year.

That's an example of living your Purpose.

We Accelerate Freedom for our clients:

We work with a client that is the world leader in personal development training. It is a large company that has had millions of customers over the years yet never focused on recovering failed payments from clients. (This is the very business Gravy does.)

These clients have to pay to attend the life-changing personal development events. So we started working with the company and now recover 68 percent of these failed payments.

Now we're *accelerating everybody's freedom*. We're reactivating dormant customers to attend life-changing events, which is helping them. We've accelerated their customers' freedom because now their lives are changed. We accelerate the financial freedom of that business because we recover millions of dollars for it.

Accelerating freedom is the outcome of what our business does.

This concept is hard to develop in writing. Because of that, you can visit dontfail.biz/purpose to help you develop your Purpose.

Look, I'll tell you straight: people's hearts are not moved by you growing your business. They don't wake up and think, "I hope I can make my owner richer today!" And if that's the only Purpose you've got going for you, they're not going to like you. And, more importantly, they are not going to work hard for you or for your customers. It's just not going to happen.

But people not only love seeing and hearing stories; they love *being part* of a bigger story. Every person at Gravy isn't just a paycheck and some work done. They help us fulfill our Purpose to provide more freedom for more people like Jamie.

At our last annual team Summit, we had a table that was empty. It represented all the open roles we have at Gravy that we want to fill. That table is one of the reasons we work so hard.

There is somebody stuck in a closet somewhere with no hope of accelerating their career. We get to be the accelerator.

We have no problem motivating our team, because the team is *self-motivated* to help others experience what they have experienced.

Do you ever wish people cared more? They will when you develop a Purpose Statement that rallies the hearts of your team.

For examples and help, go to dontfail.biz/purpose.

Developing your shared Purpose isn't the sexiest of business hacks. I get it.

But if you skip this, you will end up relying on quick-fix, B.S. hacks that work for exactly no one in the long run. Not you, not your customers, and certainly not your team.

However, if you spend time developing your shared Purpose, people will run through brick walls for your customers, for your team—and for you.

Chapter 2.4

MARINES AREN'T CONFUSED

The Foolproof Guide to Hitting All of Your Goals

I've always been fascinated by the Marine Corps. Its website copy and commercials are the absolute best at marketing to the best of the best: "The few. The proud. The Marines." ("The few." I mean, that says everything.)

Here's what I've always been the most interested in: Marines are not confused about their Mission.

In fact, they say, "Mission first, Marines always." (That means *they* don't come first. They put the Mission objective above their lives, which explains, "But your ass belongs to the Corps!" One of my favorite lines from the movie *Full Metal Jacket*.)

Everything Marines do has a clear outcome.

I learned this in person from Col. Derek Lane, who is one of a very few Marines to have achieved the rank of colonel.

His wife is Jill.

Jill and I went to high school together. We reconnected over Gravy. She started working part-time for us and rose through our ranks to become product manager.

(Jill, I salute you; the job as a Marine spouse is certainly not an easy one.)

I had the opportunity to interview Col. Lane. He said a phrase that I'll never forget. It was a quote he attributed to retired Marine Lt. Gen. Dave Beydler: "The easiest people to lead are ones who know where they are going."

That's so simple and good. And so damning.

What if all of your staff problems aren't because of your staff? What if they're because your staff doesn't know what their Mission is?

So in building Vision Clarity, after you nail your Purpose (which is why you do what you do), you must establish a current Mission.

I'm not talking about your "Mission statement." You must have a *current* Mission. This is what you're focusing on right now. It's the most important thing.

GRAVY'S MISSION: TO RETURN $1 BILLION BACK TO BUSINESSES BY 2023.

As I write this, we have returned $161 million to businesses.

Let's get laser-sharp focused on why this is important. Marines don't have jobs; they have *Missions*. It's tough to become a Marine. But you know what? It's probably tougher to get hired at your company!

So take a lesson from the Marine Corps. Don't give your team members a job. Give them a worthy Mission.

If you don't establish what the Mission is, everyone will make up their own. Because people don't want a job; they want a *Mission*.

And most owners miss this completely. I did for a season too.

As the owner, you must work with your team to develop what Mission will govern and guide their decisions.

Just like the Mission governs and guides what Marines do in the field.

This is a lot like Owner's Intent because after you define the Mission, some of your people say, "Well, what if we pivot?" or "What if the market changes?"

Guess what. That stuff *will* happen!

That's why it's called a *current* Mission. Every ninety days, we meet, look at the Mission and its strategies, and ask, "Is this still the right direction?"

At that point, if the market changes, we can start a new *current* Mission.

HOW YOUR OWNER'S INTENT WORKS WITH YOUR CURRENT MISSION

Current Mission answers every operational hiring, product, marketing, sales, and other question. When entrepreneurs ask me, "Should I raise money for my startup?" I ask them, "What's your Owner's Intent and *current* Mission?" They look at me like I'm crazy.

I think they're thinking, *Whoa, that's a lot of work to figure out. I'm going to find someone else who will give me a green light.*

You can't properly answer the question of how to raise money for your business unless you know why you own the business and what you are trying to accomplish.

It's the brutal truth, sure. But you become more willing to accept the brutal truth when you know it's what keeps you off the path of brutal failure.

FIVE STATEMENTS TO DEFINE YOUR MISSION

We used these statements to establish our current Mission. This is based on my Owner's Intent, which is "to build a company my adult kids would want to work at someday if they so choose."

1. The Mission must be bigger than we know how to accomplish.
2. The Mission must have a dollar amount and date for completion.
3. The Mission must benefit our clients.

4. The Mission must be at the core of who we are and what we do.

5. The Mission must be simple to understand.

You may have a team of three people, and your current Mission might be "to create $25,000 in recurring affiliate income by the end of next year."

Imagine how this clear Mission makes your team so much more focused and deliberate. When someone has an idea, you automatically ask, "How does this help us to accomplish our Mission?"

Your current Mission is your best friend. However, based on my experience with owners, I know that few of my readers will do this. You're probably thinking, *Oh yeah, I should do that.* But you won't.

A few of you will. For these few, for *you*, I created further training on this at dontfail.biz/mission.

It's taken me fifteen years to understand how to structure these concepts simply, and I want to teach you the shortcuts that I wish I knew all along. These would have saved me so much failure along the way.

Col. Lane's quote from Marine Lt. Gen. Dave Beydler should bother you: "The easiest people to lead are those who know where they are going."

Do you and your people clearly know what's currently most important? Do you know where you are going? Do they?

The answer is probably no.

Do the White Paper Test over Slack, via email, or at your next meeting. Ask everyone to give you their responses.

Then you'll see how much work you have to do. But when you put in the work, your current Mission will inspire your people in more ways than you can imagine. They will begin to know where they are going.

It's worth the work. Start now.

Chapter 2.5
NICE PLAQUE, ASSHOLE

How to Create a Culture People Actually Give a Sh*t About

I heard about a team member who was so sick of his company culture that he did something drastic. I don't recommend this action unless you are willing to be fired. (But it's epic.)

The company had been through some mergers. After the clashes and misery of this work environment increased to a breaking point, a leader of his division took action.

There was a framed plaque on the wall that everyone passed, day in and day out. On this plaque were the company's Core Values.

It was a bad joke.

In a rage, he grabbed the plaque off the wall, took it to his Texas home—this story is a Texas kind of story—and got out his gun. Then he went outside where he shot the hell out of it. Blew it to bits.

He put the shattered Values in a bucket and came back to work. He set up a meeting with his boss and set the bucket on his desk.

"What's this?" his boss asked.

"It's the plaque of our Values that was on the wall," he said.

"What happened to it?"

"I shot it," the man said. "Because this is what our company Values really look like."

To his surprise, the boss agreed. Then and there, they started a process to establish new, shared Values for the company.

When I talk about Core Values, a lot of leaders (and team members) roll their eyes because what's hung on the walls ain't what's happening down the halls.

Upholding Core Values is like going to the church where I grew up. You'd live however you want and claim affiliation with a church that had Values you didn't uphold. Why? Because that's what you were "supposed" to do.

It was societal pressure.

THE MOST IMPORTANT DECISION WE'VE MADE AT GRAVY

This statement might be a step too far, but I don't care, because it's how I feel.

Establishing Core Values for Gravy has been the single most important decision we've made for our culture.

Core Values are simply "how we do things around here."

Or:

- How we show up.
- How we treat people.
- What's allowed.
- What's not allowed.

If you don't establish clear Core Values, your teams become a relational Wild West.

Everyone has Core Values and lives them out anyway. Some Value is going to rise to the surface. Make it one you approve.

For an owner to enjoy spending time in the company they started, they must create clear Core Values according to which they hire, fire, and train.

Out of everything we have done, I take the most pride in this in our Core Values. In fact, we have a training for you at dontfail.biz/values, so you can dive into how to develop Core Values for your company or department.

HOW WE CREATED OUR CORE VALUES

We committed to no more than five.

I just can't expect people to remember thirteen Core Values. (Is it really "core" if it's number thirteen?)

We wrote down what pisses us off.

One of the best ways to discover what is core to you is to notice what makes you angry. When I am late or when anyone else is late to meetings, I get mad. Of course, sometimes there are good reasons for it, but generally, I want an on-time culture.

So "being on time" is the behavior I want, but we would still dig deeper.

What's the deeper meaning behind what makes us angry?

We would come back to the why test. Why does it annoy me when I'm late?

After my co-founder, Renee, and I talked about it for a while, we uncovered it's simply because I want to be *dependable*, and I want to be able to depend on others. What does dependability hinge on? It hinges on being a person of your word. If you say you will do it, you do it.

So out of this simple exercise we arrived at our first Core Value.

Core Value 1: We Do What We Say We'll Do

That's not enough, though. This is where companies mess up. They allow statements or words that mean different things to different people. But not so with you and your Values. This alone is going to put you miles ahead of your competition, even if your competition is just you right now.

We made a "does mean/doesn't mean" chart.

I learned this from my friend David. David is a wizard of building high-performing teams where culture drives performance.

He helped me see that we must be ruthlessly clear about what we mean when we elevate "We do what we say we'll do" to Value status.

So we built this:

We Do What We Say We'll Do	
DOES MEAN	**DOESN'T MEAN**
Valuing progress over perfection.	Letting perfection get in the way of necessity.
Leading with yes and knowing our limits.	People-pleasing that drives overcommitment.
Taking internal responsibility regardless of external circumstances.	Allowing external factors to become excuses.
Providing needed clarity and seeking continued clarity.	Giving or accepting ambiguous expectations.

Practically, this is what a list like this does for us:

- This time around, our hiring process is built around these specific Values and their definitions.
- If we are having a performance issue, we identify the "does mean" or "doesn't mean" that needs to be addressed.

We do ninety-day reviews and talk through each one of these. We reinforce what each person, including *me*, is doing well and where we need improvement.

We repeated this process until we had our five Core Values.

Here they are again:

We Build Others Up

DOES MEAN	DOESN'T MEAN
Appreciating others specifically.	Withholding praise of others.
Unlocking potential through belief in others.	Allowing current circumstances and results to dictate and determine our trajectory.
Confronting with care.	Diminishing others and relationships through gossip.
Valuing people as humans.	Treating people like objects.

We Do What We Say We'll Do

DOES MEAN	DOESN'T MEAN
Valuing progress over perfection.	Letting perfection get in the way of necessity.
Leading with yes and knowing our limits.	People-pleasing that drives overcommitment.
Taking internal responsibility regardless of external circumstances.	Allowing external factors to become excuses.
Providing needed clarity and seeking continued clarity.	Giving or accepting ambiguous expectations.

We Don't Take Ourselves Too Seriously

DOES MEAN	DOESN'T MEAN
Being light, loose, and approachable.	Being rigid, close-minded, and hurried.
Having a heart of work hard and play hard.	Allowing your work to define your value.
Learning from failure creates strength.	Believing failure means weakness.
Realizing accomplishments are only as good as those they benefit.	Using accomplishments to create security.
Having agility and ability to move quickly.	Being unwilling, conscious or unconscious, to let go.

We Take Initiative

DOES MEAN	DOESN'T MEAN
Seeing the opportunity.	Waiting to be told what to do.
Growing persistently.	Settling for status quo.
Starting with self leadership.	Believing growth is automatic.
Identifying and creating solutions.	Stopping at pointing out problems.

We Approach Life with Optimism

DOES MEAN	DOESN'T MEAN
Resolving that we will win in the end.	Putting limits on our possibilities.
Confronting the brutal facts of our current reality.	Keeping bad news to ourselves.
Believing the best in others.	Assuming we know all the facts.
Bringing a positive presence.	Allowing circumstances to define our attitude.

Okay, so what about you?

If you asked your team to write down your Core Values right now, how many of them would get it 100 percent right?

If I haven't convinced you yet, here are five benefits of you taking the time to do this.

FIVE BENEFITS TO ESTABLISHING YOUR COMPANY'S CORE VALUES

1. You eliminate awkward conversations.

When you have other people working on a team, people will do stuff that isn't in alignment with the behavior you prefer. Most of the time, they don't even *know* it.

So when you have clear Values, you get to talk about the *Values*, not them. The Values are the culprit. The Values are the measuring stick and what we're all working to live up to.

If I'm having an issue with someone, I print out the Values and circle the "does mean" or "doesn't mean" that's out of line. Again, we talk about that Value, not them.

However, this only works with clear Values. If the Values aren't clear, you have to correct the person. This is harder and it feels worse for everyone.

2. You disqualify most people from working with you.

When you are clear about your Values in the hiring process and you are looking for candidates to live your Values, you'll spot red flags —*fast*.

You won't get every hire right, but you will get a lot right, and you will win way more often than you'll lose.

Let's consider our Core Value of "we do what we say we'll do." If the candidate says they will send something and they don't, we notice. Because we know that once you are inside of Gravy, that is unacceptable.

3. You create a place where you actually want to work.

So many owners create companies and then don't want to be around the people. Establishing Core Values allows you to create the kind of company where you enjoy working.

4. Your customers will stay longer and pay more.

If you have a Core Value-aligned team, your customers will notice. Your service will be better. Your product team will listen better. Your people will exude togetherness and love for the customer.

This all creates a better company of customers wanting to stay longer and pay more. We have *tons* of customers trying to hire our team all the time. In fact, we love it! Attracting customers' attention is the greatest compliment ever, and it's the byproduct of people being fully alive.

5. You can't underestimate the power of the team liking each other.

When people like working with their teammates, you've nearly won the battle for motivation. Teamwork is sped up by hiring, firing, and training to the Core Values. Your team's productivity level will increase significantly with Core Values. You won't have to motivate people who like working with one another because having fun together is one of the most powerful tools for motivation.

Don't be the leader with the plaque on the wall saying what the Values are when you really don't care. You have to live by them. You have to be the core example of "how we do things around here."

The leader sets the pace and example. Yes, this means you.

Don't make me come shoot up your pretty plaque.

THE TEN-STEP PEOPLE SYSTEM

How to Create a Happy Team and Achieve Massive Results

My mom used to always say to me, "How many times am I going to have to tell you…" Then she would chase me around our house with anything she could use to spank me.

(Yes, my mom spanked me. No, I'm not ruined because of it. Yet I never thought I would be writing about childhood spankings in a business book.)

Like my mom, a parent or caregiver may have used all kinds of disciplinary measures to get you to become aware of your behavior issues and change them.

Part 2: No-B.S. Business Strategy

The same holds true with team members. You'll talk about your Core Values. You'll live them out. Yet you may still find yourself saying, "How many times do I have to tell them?"

This is what I hear all of the time from owners who painstakingly set their Owner's Intent, Purpose, Mission, and Values.

They have a meeting. They're excited and break it all down for the team. Then...crickets. Nobody cares.

You'll feel inept, like a terrible communicator. Baffled. And betrayed. You'll scream at me, "Casey! Why does nobody care?"

Then I'll let you down easy and say, "Nobody ever believes you. Ever."

When you tell your team something, they just assume it's the passing Vision of the Month. They're like your kids in that they are always looking at how you behave to see the gap between what you say and what you do. Case in point: they don't care because you've never tied their compensation to your Owner's Intent, Purpose, Mission, and Values.

Creating a world-class culture hinges on what I'm about to tell you.

HIRE, FIRE, AND WORK ACCORDING TO YOUR VALUES

Unless you are willing to fire people for not being on board with your Intent, Purpose, Mission, and Values, you will always *fail* and never *win*.

People have to know this is the most important part of the company. This is what creates your organizational DNA.

You can hire people to do jobs and get work done, but it won't be anything special unless you have a team of people rallied around your shared Vision.

Here's how we do this at Gravy:

1. THE HIRING PAGE COPY

We write copy on our hiring page to disqualify you: "It takes thirty-four hours of effort for the average person to get hired at Gravy." We try to start weeding out anyone who wants it easy, early, and often.

(Incidentally, some people think it's awesome that it takes that long to get hired—they're actually attracted by that statement. This is how you win before you even begin.)

2. APPLICATION QUESTIONS

We ask knockout questions on the application to weed out people based on our Values.

3. PHONE SCREENS

On the first phone screening, we ask questions around Values.

4. "THE GAUNTLET" INTERVIEW PROCESS

We talk about our Values but then interview people about how they have lived our style of Values in their own lives. *Past* behavior is the best predictor of *future* behavior. You can tell if people are genuinely living the Values or putting things together artificially.

5. FIRST-DAY ONBOARDING

The new hire's manager explains our Purpose, Mission, and Values. They talk about it a lot because this equals 50 percent of how the hire is going to be reviewed after ninety days.

6. NEW TEAM ORIENTATION

Once a quarter, each new round of hires gathers for four one-hour sessions with the co-founders of the company. We share the origin story of our Vision. We talk personally about our Values, and we listen as new team members talk about how they have seen them lived out in their short time with the company.

No, it's not a cult—you can believe anything you want and leave at will—but we foster the importance of living up to our Values.

7. NINETY-DAY REVIEWS

Half the review is on your alignment with our Purpose, Mission, and Values. Half is on performance. This is the ultimate reality check.

8. ALL-TEAM MEETINGS

We have weekly team meetings that everyone attends. Our Vision is always a part of this meeting, and we discuss it in many different ways. The most important thing we do is share stories of how people are living it out.

9. ANNUAL SUMMITS

We gather everyone together in person once a year. At these summits, we build our content and agenda around our Vision and culture.

10. CURIOSITY CONVERSATIONS

At any time, anyone can set up a Curiosity Conversation to have a talk about the behaviors of another person in the company. This applies to me as well.

Curiosity Conversations help newer people learn what's happening and help veterans see blind spots.

STRUCTURING FOR VALUES

The reason people don't "get" Purpose, Mission, and Values in most companies is the owner doesn't create a system for making them real.

Our magic isn't the Purpose, Mission, and Values; it's the *system* that makes them an integral part of our company culture.

When I explain this to people, they often say, "This is a lot of work."

Not really. You're thinking ahead instead of behind. It's more work to lack clarity. It's more work to try to motivate people when your fundamental culture is unmotivating.

This system creates a culture that people will run through a brick wall for.

$300 BOTTLE OF WINE

Why Reinforcing Culture Solves All Other Business Problems

I've read all kinds of books about Core Values, but rarely do they give me specific examples about how Core Values are *for real* in business. They are filled with B.S. advice instead of things you can actually sink your teeth into.

Instead, I am going to show you how to use them to:

- Attract the right team.
- Train the existing team.
- Fire the nonaligned team.

Let's jump in.

ATTRACTING TALENT

One of my most successful posts on LinkedIn is the most controversial.

I wrote about how being consistently late to virtual meetings is lazy behavior. (Note I didn't say careless or disrespectful. Just lazy.) Well, you would have thought I stole someone's firstborn kid from the cradle by how crazy some of the comments were.

Eighty percent of the responses agreed. Twenty percent thought I was the devil himself.

They vehemently told me why it's totally unreasonable to expect this.

Believe it or not, one of those people was in our hiring process. The comment made it really easy for us to question if this candidate was a fit because of our Core Values. Namely, "We do what we say we will do." Based on the comment and our "does mean/doesn't mean" chart, living out this Core Value would clearly be a challenge for this individual.

Of course, we didn't pull the plug just based on his comment. We had further conversations about our Values, and it became clear we weren't a fit for him.

This saved us tens of thousands of dollars and months of onboarding. This saved him working for the wrong company that wouldn't give him the life he wants. (Remember, this goes both ways!)

Talking openly and often about your Values will serve as a natural filtering system for attracting and repelling candidates.

We talk about our Core Values on our hiring page, on social media, during our initial phone screens, and throughout the interview process.

Core Values are everything to us, and they should be for you too.

When people are aligned with your Core Values, you can teach them just about anything. Being aligned on Core Values gives the foundation for someone becoming a great fit for our team.

Attracting the right people starts with repelling the wrong people. Talk early and often about your Core Values and what they mean. Give practical examples, and tell people the truth about how you operate.

TRAINING TALENT

We try to "catch" people doing stuff right.

The number one way we train our team on Core Values is called a #GravyBiscuit, which is a shoutout celebrating another team member in Slack (our headquarters).

Any team member can give a #GravyBiscuit at any time when we catch people living out our Core Values. It's very simple and very, *very* effective.

Here are five examples of #GravyBiscuits:

- #GravyBiscuit to Julie and Ben. For 3.5 years, I can't get the reports I want on my phone in simple and beautiful pictures—and I've never gotten them real time and right.

Welp, they've done it. Thank you for absolutely living the Value of "We Do What We Say We Will Do" and delivering these.

- #GravyBiscuit to Sally for living out the Core Value of "We Take Initiative." Sally has taken full ownership of her roster of clients. She has admitted when she has made any mistake and has taken those learnings and made herself better. She has amped up her Slack game, and she is always bringing a positive presence!

- #GravyBiscuit to Rachel for living out our Core Value of "We Approach Life with Optimism." She's recently dealt with change in such a positive way. She always brings a positive presence. She knows that we *will* win in the end, and I absolutely love being able to work more closely with her.

- #GravyBiscuit to Mark. He lived out "We Don't Take Ourselves Too Seriously" by learning that failure creates strength (and knowledge).

- #GravyBiscuit to Dave. Aside from absolutely crushing it, the man still finds time to help anyone who needs it. This embodies "We Build Others Up."

Why does this work?

Because people repeat what's rewarded.

Notice that the number one reward system inside of Gravy doesn't cost money. It only costs us our words and requires us to pay attention to people and our Values. Notice also I said this is the number one way we train. Training shouldn't feel like a drag. It should feel like a Gravy Biscuit.

You wouldn't believe how people will run through a brick wall for you if you positively reinforce what they do right.

However, there will be times when people behave in a way that's counter to our culture.

This leads to what I've established as a Curiosity Conversation.

WINE NOT?

One time, we hired this guy, and the next week he was on a business trip with us. He came as a recommendation from an existing team member. Because of that, we kinda stepped over some of the hiring process. (Yeah, I know. Talk about failing before you even begin.)

On the trip, we were at dinner at the finest Italian restaurant in San Francisco, all on Gravy's tab.

(As you know by reading this book, I'm not really into fancy things. I don't enjoy going to white-tablecloth restaurants. But we had a big win that day. The team picked this place to celebrate, so I went along with it.)

Sitting at dinner, our new hire kept calling over the sommelier. I noticed he just talked and talked, as if he had no clue that the server might have other customers and duties to attend to. He was so pretentious that the sommelier himself said to the entire table, "He sure does think he knows a lot about wine, doesn't he?"

Now that's a Scud missile comment! You would think at that point the new hire would back down, but he didn't. In fact, he *doubled down*.

He cornered the poor waiter again and then whispered something to him. Finally, the new hire sent the sommelier over to me with a bottle of wine. In front of the table, he said, "Mr. Graham, it's up to you, but he would like to order this bottle for the table."

Everyone was looking at me. I took a gander at this menu item. It was a $300 bottle of wine.

Let me make this clear: I'm 100 percent fine with ordering even a $2,000 bottle of wine if that floats your boat. But this wasn't our new hire's boat. This was the Gravy boat, and he was a week in acting like a celebrity at the Ritz-Carlton.

The team and waitstaff were fed up with babysitting his ego, and I was fed up with being put on the spot in front of my staff. I remember texting my co-founder Renee (because she wasn't there) and saying, "This guy is probably not going to make it."

I was really peeved by this incident, and it surprised me. I didn't know why I was so upset. After all, I truly am fine with people ordering nice things. After a lot of reflection, I realized it wasn't the "nice thing." It was the not-so-nice behavior behind it all. It was the way he was treating the sommelier and his lack of self-awareness that got to me.

I kept thinking, *If he treats the waitstaff this way—over something that doesn't matter at all—how will he treat his direct reports when something does matter?* Then I remembered my Owner's Intent. (Remember it?)

To create a company my adult children would
want to work at if they so choose.

I asked myself in that moment, *Would I want my daughter working for him?*

Hell no, I thought. But why?

As we returned from the trip, I asked Renee why this set me off so bad. She said, "Your personal Values were violated, and our company Core Values were violated as well."

So I pulled out our company Values, and one of them is "We don't take ourselves too seriously."

Well, bingo. He had taken himself *quite* seriously, and at the expense of others, both personally and financially. I couldn't sweep this under the rug.

So what do you do when Values are violated?

You have a Curiosity Conversation.

During the call with him, I brought up the incident and the wine order. I remember it like it was yesterday. His reaction was even more problematic. He couldn't believe this was even a big deal.

I tried to help him see how what he displayed was pretentious behavior that didn't show consideration for other people, and I told him that wasn't tolerated with us. Putting people on the spot in public is not okay. I wanted to coach him—there are certainly people who can be coached and grow past behavior like this—but he couldn't even see how it was an issue. When we got off the call, I looked at Renee, and we just shook our heads.

He was an absolute fit, just not with Gravy. We believe everyone fits or adds to an organization. But it might not necessarily be at Gravy.

We parted ways with the wine gentleman. What I've learned is that being willing to absorb and correct a temporary hire failure sets us up for wins down the road. But only if we learn from them.

THE THREE-STEP CORE VALUES CURIOSITY CONVERSATION

You aren't always going to nail hiring. But *when* (not if) you don't get it right and have to have a Curiosity Conversation, there are ways to do it well. Here's how to have that sit-down.

1. I CIRCLE THE VALUE WE ARE TALKING ABOUT ON PAPER.

Never be vague. I print out a piece of paper. Even if it's virtual, I will hold it up and circle which part of the Values we are talking about. The more specific you are, the more you'll help them see where they have a blind spot.

Paper works well because it moves the conversation off the person and onto an object. I point at the paper and talk about *it*, not the team member. You never want anyone to feel attacked.

2. WE WRITE DOWN EXACTLY WHAT THE ACTION STEPS ARE TO CORRECT THIS.

After the conversation, we send an email to all the parties involved and recap the necessary action steps to align with the Value.

This can't be vague. You must be clear in the email and ask for a response so you know they understand it and agree. If they don't agree, you must have another conversation to clarify the issue.

3. WE SET A TIMELINE TO REGROUP.

Usually, we'll set a time to regroup and discuss how things are progressing within thirty days.

If things aren't going well, it's likely time to drop the F-bomb. No, not that one. Even worse.

It's time to fire.

RED ROVER, RED ROVER, LET'S GET THAT FIRE OVER

This is the worst chapter in the book. I've made more mistakes with exits and firings than any other part of business. It sucks to even write about how much I've messed up here. I'll share what we've learned and how you can *not* screw up as much as we did.

So I'm going to shoot it to you straight. Remember how I said some chapters were going to be heavier than others? Well, this one feels like an elephant. It's the elephant in the room that you *have* to talk about if you want to win where others fail.

Because overall, Values are the most practical tool for building a great team that's aligned and that cares. It's how you hire well and how you fire well.

Having strong Core Values is why firing hurts. Not only because of the personal pain, but there are all kinds of legal ramifications as well. I'm not an HR expert. Their perspective is different from the owner's perspective.

SIDE NOTE

By the way, have you ever been to an HR conference?

Good gracious, they go *wild*!

Maybe it's because they have to keep everyone else in line all the time, but they're like parents getting away from the kids for a weekend. The HR and finance people always surprise me at two in the morning when Ginuwine's "My Pony" plays.

Most firings were my fault from the beginning.

Please, save yourself and the world some pain and learn from my mistakes.

TOP FIVE FIRING MISTAKES I'VE MADE THAT I DON'T WANT YOU TO MAKE

1. BEWARE OF DUAL RELATIONSHIPS

There was a period of time that I was living in a great neighborhood. It had a strong community.

I became acquainted with a fantastic neighbor. He was the kind of guy you want by your side when you are completing a tough work project on your house. Over time, we started talking about work. I joked about recruiting him for a while. Then it moved from joking to real talks of him joining our company.

Here's the problem: Dual Relationships happen when you have two different kinds of relationships with the same person. In this example, it's neighbor/work recruit.

But for you, it could happen in many ways. It could be:

- A family member or a spouse who joins your business.
- A church friend who you hire.
- Your best friend who becomes a director.

Regardless, it creates a Dual Relationship. And regardless, it's a problem.

You're not objective. You are too connected and friendly. You care too much about this person. Or even yourself. You like being around them, so you think, *I'll like being around them at the office. They'll add so much!* Famous last words.

So we hired my neighbor. *He is a stellar neighbor,* I thought. *I bet he will be a stellar team member!*

Well, long story short, he just wasn't. We ended up having to part ways, and it was a messy disaster.

Frankly, I'm glad we ended the business relationship. But because it was a Dual Relationship, it ruined an entire relationship that didn't have to be ruined.

You see, when you enter a Dual Relationship, you can never go back to the relationship you had. You are aware of a new side to the person, and they see a new side to you.

It's a lot like dating. When you're just friends, the person's a blast, which is why you want to bring them closer into your life. But you can't date and be friends. You become too close. We all know this, yet we often make the same mistake in business too.

I blame myself for creating this Dual Relationship with my neighbor. However, I don't blame myself for it not being a good fit. That's just how life works sometimes. You have to try it out, and sometimes you're just not a fit for Gravy. (In fact, even the most amazing people aren't always.)

If you're going to ignore this advice and mix two relationships, you must be clear about this with:

- A contract.
- An up-front conversation.
- A no-holds-barred dialogue about all the *bad* outcomes that are possible.

Now if I have any Dual Relationships, I start by saying, "I am probably going to have to fire you." This way, we have that conversation on the front end. We walk through the nasty outcomes that can happen in business, and we talk about it openly and honestly.

No B.S., no blinders. No wishful thinking. It's the B.S. that will get you into the mess in the first place. The more direct and candid you are, the better chance you have at actually making it work in business and outside of business.

If you have any Dual Relationships right now that you need to clean up, let them read this chapter, and then sit down to talk through it. You will not regret it.

But you will regret *not* firing people who need to go.

This brings me to number two.

2. BEWARE OF HANGING ON TOO LONG

This may sound brutal, but it's more brutal for everyone to try to make something work that isn't going to work. You may think you are hanging on for them, but in reality, you are likely hanging on for you.

Fire people fast. Someone is reading this and needs to hear this.

You think it's going to be awful, and it's going to hurt them and you. You think it's a huge deal. It is a big deal, of course. But sometimes, you just have to fire people. Not because it's the easy thing to do but because it's the *right* thing to do. For them and for you.

The number one way to know if I need to make a decision on firing someone is the cell phone test—if their number comes up on my phone and I want to avoid them. There is always a reason I want to avoid them. Ninety percent of the time it's a Core Value misalignment, and it's draining to be in the same workspace with them.

Regardless, quit waiting. Have the conversation now. Even if it's not to fire them, you must be honest and at the very least continue having those Curiosity Conversations.

I've waited, and when you wait, you drag yourself and your team into Miseryland where you ride the Anxiety Roller Coaster all day long. Muster up the courage and go talk to them. Do it now.

3. BEWARE OF ANYTHING VERBAL

My mentor says, "Good paper keeps good friends." I used to be the king of messing up all hiring because I would just say stuff instead of having it all written down.

If you remember nothing else, *never* hire anyone without a written job profile that describes the activities, responsibilities, and results required for the role.

Always list all promises. Always list all financial conversations. If anything changes, amend it immediately.

I see more issues arise from people having verbal agreements than anything else. "I thought you said..." the person says.

"I didn't say that!" you say.

You see, it's just a mess. People hear what they want to hear.

If you have teams and you need to clean this up, give them this chapter, and tell them to get mad at me. I'm used to people being mad at me, so bring it on.

If you need to start over with your team and write it all down, do so.

You can go to dontfail.biz/people for examples of how to create clean and clear job profiles. We included twenty-five profiles for you to use as templates.

4. BEWARE OF COACHING AVOIDANCE

I see too many leaders want to fire people before coaching them. That's just dumb, unless they are stealing money or something unethical.

I truly believe most people want to do well and will adjust, but a lot of leaders don't do well with offering feedback.

Here is the phrase that pays: "Are you open to some feedback?"

Never give feedback unless they give you permission. If you do, it will be taken as judgment, and people rebel from that.

I have a 100 percent yes to that question, and I've found most people want you to be radically honest with them.

Here's the point: you should be having these conversations all the time, and people should be able to have them with you. If you are avoiding giving feedback and just want to fire someone, that's on you. I've done this before.

Here is one more tip the B.S. gurus won't give you: after you get permission to give feedback, say, "I notice," and "I prefer."

"*I notice* you tend to be the first one to speak in all meetings and usually talk for a while. In our next meeting, *I'd prefer* we let others

speak first so we can listen and not dominate the conversation."
Ninety-nine percent of people will accept this and work on it.

Problem solved. No B.S. required.

5. BEWARE OF WORKING AROUND PEOPLE

There are some people who are fine people. If they call you, you
happily answer. However, you are working around them.

- You create systems around them.
- You have staff talking around them.
- You try to fit them into the overall culture.

These people are really good for lifestyle businesses, but if you
are going to be scaling a company like we are doing at Gravy, you
don't want to work around anyone.

The reason is that it says to everyone, "Some people can do whatever they want." This will create a toxic culture.

If you are working around someone, you need to be honest with
yourself about why.

I had a team member once who was really good. The really bad
part? I allowed workarounds for them for a long time because when
we were starting out, they were the only one in a certain department.

I allowed things I wouldn't allow from anyone else. This created a
breaking point as we started to scale, and ultimately, it worked out
great on their exit. They are now thriving and killing it, but usually
it doesn't work out that well.

This chapter is messy. Because when you have people and money mixed, it's messy.

So learn from my mistakes. Learn how to win where I've failed and save yourself—and the people around you—from more pain than is vital for growth—both theirs and, ultimately, yours and your business's.

P.S. Go to dontfail.biz/people to learn actual firing strategies and how to coach people up. You'll thank me when you get this right.

Chapter 2.9
SIZE DOESN'T MATTER; CLARITY DOES

Purpose, Mission, and Values drive everything.

Even if you are a solopreneur, the clearer you become on these three intangibles—to the point that you make them *real*—the better your life will be.

This part is over, and the book is about to get super practical. It'll be as wild as an HR conference. You'll see how Gravy operates.

I'm not saying what you're about to read is the Small Business Gospel. (It could be dead wrong if you're using this book to pass an HR test or writing a paper about how successful companies operate.) However, it works for us.

If you're anything like us, you'll soon be able to leverage some of our hard-earned, no-B.S. approach to create an amazing place to work.

PART 3

NO-B.S.
BUSINESS HACKS

"You have everything you need to
build something far bigger
than yourself."

—Seth Godin

By now, you have likely learned more about yourself, your drive, and your motives than you may have imagined.

Now let's get down to the business of business. Everything you have ever wanted in business and in life is right on the other side of you taking massive action from your massive intentions. Specifically, from your Owner's Intent.

It's time to move from passive thoughts to—you guessed it—*massive action*.

In this section, we'll dive deep into practical steps you can take today to achieve the success you want in your business tomorrow. Yes, some may consider these "hacks." I don't. In fact, I call it your how-to guide for cutting out the B.S. fluff and committing to what actually works.

From creating a Slack channel around celebrating failures (#failebration) to learning how to build and leverage your personal brand and your team's brand on LinkedIn, this section will satisfy your competitive spirit and your tactical itch.

Buckle up, friends. It's time for a no-B.S. hack-a-thon.

Chapter 3.1

GUTSY MOVE

Trusting Your Biggest Strategic Advantage

Gravy's no-B.S. story attracted a top dog with high cost and a big ego. Sixty days in, he and I stood face-to-face, and my gut knew (two months too late) that he wasn't a good fit for our company.

This highly talented recruit had gone from someone I was so happy to get on our team to an internal nightmare. He'd left his fourteen-year career to join my little startup. He talked about that a lot. He talked about what he was sacrificing to believe in Gravy.

To believe in *me*.

Situations like this make you wish hiring could be like a one-night stand. Instead, it's a messy marriage with a prenup.

He created massive anxiety for me. My gut told me something was off, but like in a bad relationship, you avoid that voice in your head.

I remember thinking, *Maybe I'm just the crazy one. I have my own stuff too. I'm sure it's just me who feels this way.*

I mean, isn't this what we are supposed to do as entrepreneurs? Create a story for people to believe in? Cast a big Vision to get powerful people to join us and defy the odds with them? How could doing the right thing by hiring this star-studded maverick talent be wrong?

As if this wasn't weighty enough, our kids do activities together, and we are in a lot of the same circles, with many connections and common friends. A Dual Relationship rears its ugly head again.

My gut was still saying, *This is not right.* For the next thirty days, I worried about him and my team. Finally, after two glasses of wine in San Diego with one of my best friends who knows us both, I confessed, "I think I messed up bringing him on."

Instead of swatting away my misgivings and making me feel better, which is what you want to hear after a confession, he just looked at me and agreed. *Dang,* I thought. *I guess I did mess up.*

I asked my co-founder, Renee, the level-headed leader. Her comment was even more ruthless. "I told you not to hire him," she said.

Now it wasn't just my gut. But how could I have been so behind the eight ball? First, someone totally outside my company said it wasn't the right fit. Then my right hand said she knew it all along, and I'd forgotten that I hadn't listened to her!

Ninety days in, and I was going to have to remove a once-promising hire who'd left his secure career where he'd been doing fine to enhance *my* company—and it was all my dumb idea in the first place. Not to mention, he had an ego the size of Texas. This was going to *suck*.

Firing someone (who it was your idea to hire) is like being nauseous and, after a long time negotiating the pain, *finally* vomiting. Even though you're writhing in agony, throwing up is so bad that you try to make it through your illness without doing it.

Unfortunately, my gut wanted to upchuck. *If you don't do this now, you will lose the other top people,* it said. *He is not a culture fit.*

I set up the meeting. It was really nasty. I don't think I handled all of it right. I was really terrified of the situation because I wasn't just losing a staff member but my local reputation as a businessman if he shared publicly where we disagreed.

Firing is not for the thin-skinned. But my gut told me it was the right move.

I sat down with him a week later and listened to him read a letter to me about how I'm an immoral liar. He even skewered me with my Owner's Intent.

"You say you want to build a company your kids would want to work at. They wouldn't be proud to work at a company that treats people like this."

I listened and learned. I knew he was embarrassed and in pain. His letter didn't hurt me; in fact, I expected it.

What I did *not* expect was who else I learned from that day. Five random team members called me. This never happens. Each one said, "Thank you for what you did. We were all wondering why he was still here." Wow. I truly was the last to know!

No-B.S. leaders have to clean up their own stuff some of the time. Yet we tend to see things in a certain way and have a sixth sense about certain things. It's a gut instinct.

In retrospect, it was relatively painless for my team members to be in touch with their guts and know what was really going on. They only saw the downside of this inappropriate hire. They didn't have skin in the game with him like I did. But they did have skin in the game of our *culture*—so they knew exactly what was wrong and how it was affecting them.

They were like the stomach, trying to squeeze out what's unhealthy. I was like the brain, deciding whether I'd accept the pain of throwing him up.

I had a lot on the line with this guy. So it was harder for me to sense the truth of my instincts. I needed a wine party in San Diego and a wake-up from Renee to *believe* what my gut was telling me. To trust what us no-B.S. leaders have as a strategic advantage.

The problem with doing things by gut is that it says to do things that are uncomfortable. It's, in fact, *gutsy* and often the opposite of what everyone else does in the same circumstance. It's definitely opposite of what the Business Porn gurus tell you to do.

I'm hesitant to write this chapter because I'm still hesitant to trust my gut. I second-guess my gut instinct, even after forty years of it usually being right.

I'm going to tell you to trust your gut as you lead, *even though* I still struggle to listen when my gut is yelling at me.

Look, the first step in doing this is admitting you have a problem, right? Well, the first step in trusting your gut is simply being aware your gut is *yelling*. You'll know because it'll probably be painful in some way.

Your gut is that voice that says stuff like:

- "Fire them!" before everyone else starts telling you to do it.
- "Don't take that money!" when everyone is telling you it's a good deal.
- "It's time to double down!" when people feel like the risk is too high.
- "Don't take on this client!" when it's good money and you need it.
- "Be careful of this partnership!" when it seems like a win-win at first.
- "We aren't close enough to our clients!" when your team thinks you are.
- "Fight that competitor!" when most people would just play nice and lay down with the big dogs out of fear of being crushed.

GRAVY'S GUT REACTION TO THE EARLY DAYS OF COVID-19

When COVID-19 hit our world, we had no idea what would happen with Gravy. It was one of the scariest times of our lives as business owners.

I remember avoiding what was happening for a week. I felt like I had my head in the sand while I saw the NBA shut down and the canceling of the Masters golf tournament and the NCAA basketball tournament.

It built up in me. Suddenly, while staring at my lake as if it was any other Sunday, I remember the new reality of the pandemic hitting me. *Oh crap,* I thought, feeling like I'd gotten hit was an electric jolt. *This is real, and it could kill us and our clients.*

My gut started *screaming.* It said something I wasn't expecting: *When everyone runs out, we run in. We're built for this.*

Until this point in our (short) company history, we were completely unknown in the market. We had some traction, but it was niche traction. Virtually nobody would miss us if a pandemic made us go "poof."

Nobody may have known us *outside* Gravy, but nobody truly knew what was happening *inside* of Gravy. Our culture had been white-hot for a year. We were building a winning identity with our people, and we had a lot of foxhole momentum. Meaning, the people of Gravy would kick ass for each other at the drop of a hat.

So in response to COVID-19, I wrote this email that Sunday night by the lake.

Gravy + COVID-19
6 messages

Casey Graham
To: All Team <■■■■■■■■■■■>
Bcc: Renee Weber <■■■■■■■■■■■>

A lot is out of our control right now.

As the world is in unique times, I wanted to let you know what the next few weeks would look like here at Gravy.

We will send a weekly email to update you as all of this unfolds.

Here is the best article I've seen that summarizes this virus & risks: https://www.vox.com/future-perfect/2020/3/12/21172040/coronavirus-covid-19-virus-charts

1. Gravy is Virtually Open

I've always said, "Slack is our Headquarters."

We are a virtual business...and thank goodness we are.

We are set up to shine during these times as a guide to our clients we serve & other businesses.

- Our hours will be our normal business hours.
- We are open.
- There will be no in-person meeting requirements.
- ATL-Peeps: WeWork & Vickery offices are open but you are not required to be there
- Team meetings & operations will flow as normal this week.

2. Gravy is be Flexible

With kids being out of school & a lot of change with "normal", we want to be full of flexibility.

Here's what that means...

Your scheduel may look different this week & that's okay.

Here's what we ask each person to do...

- Create a personalized work plan with your direct report by Monday at 9AM
- If you will be financially impacted by childcare costs, Kacie & I have decided to personally help you with costs. We don't want you to be stressed about money & we ask you to work with your direct report on financial impact. Each situation will be different so we will work case by case to help you feel no impact.
- Darby is sitting here saying, "Dad, tell the local people to hire me to help them." So, there's that. Lol

3. Gravy will Serve

We are on a mission to return $1 Billion back to businesses.

During this time, our clients will be nervous of the economic impact.

The customers we are recovering are scared.

So, we will serve with empathy & helpfulness.

We will be a light in this dark time. I'm preparing a message for Gravy clients & how we will be operating at full capacity & full empathy for customers.

So, to be clear (cause y'all know I love clarity):

- Your expectations to your metrics & clients remain the same.
- We will increase communication to clients this week & use this time to be a strong leader, not a fearful follower.

Listen, we are Gravy.

Our culture was built for times like this. We will win this week & be a model for how to serve in times like this.

My #1 filter for this week is…"how would I want my kid's company to respond during a time like this?"

Hopefully, the flexibility and personalized work plans will be a helpful way to approach this week.

Your friend,
Casey Thomas Graham

(Notice my filter? My Owner's Intent guided my gut.)

My gut was saying, *This is our time to take ground. This is our time to show everyone how Gravy serves. The tide has gone out on us all, and it has shown that we are naked. We must hand out towels, not just stand around and look for our own.*

Not many knew it, but this was the most opposite gut instinct of my life.

It said that we would approach this time with clarity and confidence—regardless of our own demise or peril.

1. We continued to serve.
2. We became a light in a dark time.
3. We went from unknown to one of the most recognized brands on LinkedIn.
4. We went from a low cash balance to raising money in the middle of the scariest time in many of our lives.

Your gut will ask you to do things that will cost you. *Do it anyway.*

Your gut will tell you to look like a fool. *Trust it anyway.*

Your gut will terrify you. *Embrace it anyway.*

Your gut is your strategic advantage.

Yes, it's an actual strategy, which gives you an advantage in the market because you are willing to take action to zig when everyone else zags.

What's your gut asking you to do right now?

NO-B.S. HACKS

No-B.S. Hack 1: Trust your gut.

RESULTS OVER ACTIVITY

The Only Economy that Matters

The secret to time management is to spend time in chunks when and where you have energy. Other than that, I think managing time is a waste of time.

Time management is for people who live in the Activity Economy, which is built on getting a paycheck every two weeks for staying relatively busy and likable in your job.

If you remain a member of the Activity Economy and just like that—*voila*—money magically appears in your bank account, then part of what you're working for is security. Its luxury, and its price, is remaining active whether you're productive or not.

Entrepreneurs can't afford the Activity Economy—the economy that runs off unproductive activity.

Enter the Results Economy, which is built on taking action on the right activities at the right time that produce the right result: money.

I see too many entrepreneurs spending their time on activities they think need to be done but don't. Because nothing really matters unless you can make money.

So I created a saying we live by at Gravy: action creates traction.

Here is the principle: money walks. When I went to work for myself, I looked at my wife and then-one-year-old daughter. In that moment, it hit me: I had to bring home *actual* money in two weeks.

So as an entrepreneur for the last fourteen years, I've lived in the Results Economy. I've learned that busyness doesn't pay very well.

That's why our team at Gravy lives in the Results Economy. You will not receive a magical paycheck every two weeks if you aren't producing money or results that will lead to money.

THE DOLLAR MENU

I once had a sales rep who told me about all of his weekly activity. However, he wasn't selling anything. So I did what any good owner does: I took the rep to McDonald's, of course.

At the drive-through, I ordered a one-dollar cheeseburger. We pulled up to the window, and I said, "Mr. Rob is going to pay for this one-dollar cheeseburger by sharing with you all the activity he did this week."

The lady looked at me like I was crazy. Then at "Mr. Rob." He was frozen. I sat quietly to make it more awkward. Then I finally pulled out a dollar and paid for the cheeseburger.

I listen to so many entrepreneurs talk about all the people they are meeting with and all the activity they are doing. How much do they make with that? If they're lucky, enough for a Happy Meal.

As we drove back, he got the point: his activity didn't matter. The only thing that mattered was getting a result to get money to keep us in business and to keep him getting a paycheck.

Would I be true to my Owner's Intent and do this drive-through stunt to jump-start my own kids if they worked in my company? Of course I would! Incidentally, I learned this hack after using it on them.

Don't let your team live in the Activity Economy. Don't be a magical money provider to anyone.

Financial expert Dave Ramsey says, "Your pay raise will be effective when you are." I wholeheartedly agree.

Tie every position to results that will buy you and your kids a cheeseburger. Only then will you be in business long enough to weather the storms, hand out towels to those who need them, and have *actual* money to do all the things you want to do.

NO-B.S. HACKS

No-B.S. Hack 1: Trust your gut.

No-B.S. Hack 2: Live in the Results Economy.

Chapter 3.3
FLUSH THE TOILET
*How to Get Rid of the Sh*t Holding You Back*

Here's some unasked-for advice: go to counseling.

Yes, you. Yes, I said it.

Don't skip this now because you think it's too woo-woo. We all have hidden pain to process that is holding us back personally and professionally.

While I'm at it, go exercise. We all have to take care of our bodies so we don't fall apart.

That covers the internal and the external. You might hate both counseling and exercise, but they should matter to you.

I used to work out with another business owner every day at noon. We'd grab our weights and talk as we got our workout gear ready. As a fellow business owner, he could relate to business owner stress in the same no-B.S. way that I could.

"Casey," he'd say with his signature grin at the beginning of the workout, "let's flush the toilet."

And we did. It was the best hour of the day.

Your body doesn't get rid of stress. It takes the stress of you fighting against the world and bottles it up, which isn't healthy.

So you have two options:

1. Live with it.
2. Release it.

Option one will depress you, hurt you, and then kill you. Option two will allow you to live and operate at maximum effectiveness. I choose option two.

But this isn't a one-time deal. Stress needs to be flushed consistently. I've tried a few ways before, but here are two of the main ways I've landed on that actually work well.

COUNSELING/THERAPY

You can go online or you can go in person, but one way or the other, just go. Go process your personal life and your business life with someone who can help you with your thoughts and feelings.

Case in point: have you ever met someone who got older but didn't get better? That will be you if you don't go to counseling.

Self-awareness is key for your personal transformation and success in life. Most humans are not that self-aware. We need help to see who we are and what we do—just like the sales guy at the

McDonald's drive-through I talked about in the Results Economy chapter. You will also need someone to help you process the anger you feel as you take all the shots being an entrepreneur.

Let me say it to you straight: if you don't build self-awareness, you will ruin your life. You think you won't, but you will. If you are reading this thinking, *I have self-awareness,* it means you don't.

The scariest leaders are leaders who believe they are self-aware. We all become hard and cynical without outside perspective and processing help.

This will be new terrain for many, so try reaching out to your healthcare provider to go about the process.

EXERCISE

I've met very few successful entrepreneurs who don't have a physical outlet where they can let their minds rest. It doesn't matter how you do it, but be like Nike (yes, you know the phrase).

If you don't stress your body, the world will. It's up to you to choose good stress or killer stress.

When you exercise, you're changing how your body functions at the cellular level. You're getting stronger, achieving a goal, and helping your energy levels and immune system.

If you do nothing else today, do this. Create a schedule for counseling and exercise. Your entire life will become better because the entirety of you will become better, inside and out.

NO-B.S. HACKS

No-B.S. Hack 1: Trust your gut.

No-B.S. Hack 2: Live in the Results Economy.

No-B.S. Hack 3: Flush the toilet.

Chapter 3.4
WISHFUL THINKING
Why You Need to Retire Now

Work will always fill the space you give it. Give it your time, it'll take it. Work doesn't discriminate. It eats all time equally: honeymoon time, family time, personal time, father-and-son time, mother-and-daughter time, meditation time, the good times, and the bad times—work eats it all.

When you are lying on your deathbed, I guarantee you will not think, *I wish I would have hustled harder on that tech platform company I was a part of. If I'd only worked more hours to finish it faster, we'd have made more money.*

Come on, people. We are better than this.

Nothing is worse than having regrets on your deathbed. That's why you spend your life working fiercely on your Owner's Intent—not just in business but all areas of your life. Owner's Intent means you own your entire life with intention.

It means your family plan is no less important than your business plan. Ask yourself now: what is your hustle eating that you don't want it to eat? If you have made it this far in the book, you obviously care about creating a business that serves you and doesn't dominate your life because it's in tune with your Values.

Let me shoot it to you straight: quit sacrificing your life on the altar of business success. You might not feel it until it's too late, especially because so many people we laud and emulate *live* to sacrifice everything for work. They live to keep up with what popular culture tells them is important, ignoring what is *honestly* important to them.

I'm about to make you ask how honest you are.

The quality of your life will be found in the quality of your relationships. I once read this survey of people on their deathbeds in Australia about what they most regret.

THE FIVE THINGS PEOPLE REGRET MOST ON THEIR DEATHBEDS

1. I WISH I'D HAD THE COURAGE TO LIVE A LIFE TRUE TO MYSELF.

Developing your Owner's Intent allows you to be courageous and live true to yourself.

And if you choose an Owner's Intent to "change the world and work all the time and have my kids hate me," that's fine, but don't live that way unless you *choose* it.

Like in the movie *Ad Astra*, when a long-lost astronaut (Tommy Lee Jones) tells his son (Brad Pitt) about how career-minded he is: "I never cared about you, or your mother, or any of your small ideas…I knew this [Mission] would widow your mother and orphan you, but I found my destiny. So I abandoned my son."

Ouch. But *honest*.

Living your true life is simply deciding on the things you want to experience with the people you want to experience them with and then figuring out how your business can propel you to those experiences.

I see so many people thinking they will live their true lives *later*. That truly is a lie. However, you can live however you want *now* if you refuse to let your business be the excuse that steals your life away.

2. I WISH I HADN'T WORKED SO HARD.

You just have to make a decision to work less.

I had a business owner friend call me recently and say, "Can you help me work four days a week instead of five?"

"Sure. It's pretty simple," I said.

"No, it's not," she snapped back. "I have so many meetings and structures and systems to change. We have to help our team see the reason why, and all of this is hard."

"No, it isn't," I replied. "You are making up a story about it being hard because you really don't want to do it."

"Yes, I do!" she said. "That's why I called you."

"No, you don't," I repeated again. "You don't need consulting on how to do it. You just need to do it. It's like a diet. You truly don't need any new information. Just close your business on Friday, Saturday, and Sunday right now."

"Ughhhhh," she groaned.

I said it once, and I'll say it again: work will *always* fill the space you give it. You do not have to overwork to be successful. Just the opposite. You have to make a *decision* to work less.

If you are reading this and say that you are late to your kids' activities because of work, I call B.S. You are late because you prioritize work over your kids.

Like the long-lost astronaut said, "I never cared about you or any of your small ideas…I found my destiny. So I abandoned my son."

Harsh? Nope. It's the truth for you, and it's been the truth for me too.

You know the saying "guns don't kill people; people kill people"? Same is true for work. Work never destroyed a relationship. People destroy relationships.

You are simply saying, "I want to have a relationship with my work because it gives me more pleasure than my other relationships."

No judgment. Let's just call it what it is.

If you want more pleasure out of your relationships, the solution might be counseling, not less work. And if too much work is the problem, choose to work less and avoid the deathbed regret.

3. I WISH I'D HAD THE COURAGE TO EXPRESS MY FEELINGS.

I have nothing to add here. If you need help with self-expression, get it. You won't regret it.

4. I WISH I HAD STAYED IN TOUCH WITH MY FRIENDS.

Have you ever faked a friendship? That's why I call Facebook *Fakebook.*

It's a fake way to feel connected to humans. I don't think it's some evil choice, but I believe it's inoculated us from creating *real* friendships.

Listen, if you don't do anything with this book but put it down right now, text your friends, and convince them to go on a trip together in the next six months, it will be the greatest joy of your life—and mine.

(In fact, do it now, and then let me know when you do. I'm on LinkedIn.)

Friends determine the quality and direction of your life. Set up a weekly friend lunch now. Don't let another day go by without creating that get-together.

This is what you will regret: not nurturing friendships. Go back up and read number four. Notice people didn't say they wished they'd stayed in touch with family.

Friendship is the most unique relationship on earth. When you are family, you *must* have relationships because of blood. When you are married, you *promised* to be in a relationship.

When you work together, it's through necessity as colleagues, employers, and team members.

But a friendship is two humans mutually agreeing to be in a relationship for no benefit except that they enjoy each other.

My friendships have been the most important relationships to keep me going—and encouraged—on my business owner journey. I spend an enormous amount of time and money with them.

One of my personal goals with Gravy is to make enough money to buy the 276 acres beside our farm and gift it to three of our best friends. Then I'll pay to build their houses on it. I know it sounds crazy, but that's just who we are.

Don't let your business steal your friendships. You won't get together "sometime." Schedule it now. Don't die with this regret.

Your business will never love you, but your friends will. Choose to nurture what matters.

5. I WISH I HAD LET MYSELF BE HAPPIER.

This happiness we search for in vain comes from living out the other four regrets. If you don't have those regrets, you'll be happier.

There *is* a better way to live. More often than not, we can't get there by ourselves. This is why counseling is so crucial for anyone who wants to live their life as a no-B.S. business owner.

THE FIVE WAYS COUNSELING HELPS YOU LIVE WITHOUT REGRET

1. It helps you to create the space to live courageously, fully, and happily.
2. It helps you to work less hard.
3. It helps you to express your feelings.
4. It helps you to be in touch with your friends.
5. It helps you to be happier.

So you can die happy, and you can die fulfilled.

Remember the guy in Part 1 who sold for billions but didn't have purpose? Don't do that. Quit lying about your business needing you. The reality is that you need your business to make you *feel* needed. But one day, you'll regret it.

I can hear you now: "Okay, Mr. Purpose-Driven Guy, I've heard the deathbed scare talk before; what should I do?"

Glad you asked! Take the top five regrets we just discussed and do the opposite now, while you have time. Are you going to keep lying to yourself, or will you choose to lead and live differently in your business and retire now?

NO-B.S. HACKS

No-B.S. Hack 1: Trust your gut.

No-B.S. Hack 2: Live in the Results Economy.

No-B.S. Hack 3: Flush the toilet.

No-B.S. Hack 4: Retire now.

Chapter 3.5

(SLING)SHOTS FIRED

Screw Them and Their Way of Doing Things

What I'm about to share with you is the only reason any company I've started has ever grown.

It's the one chapter of this book that if you get wrong or don't do, you are guaranteed to get massively stuck in business. No B.S.

It starts with a teenager who fought a giant to save his country.

The famous biblical story of David and Goliath is one of the greatest examples of how an undertrained underdog can leverage the low position for strength.

Everyone thought David was crazy. Everyone thought he would die. Everyone thought he should fight the battle their way.

King Saul wanted him to put on his own kingly armor and wield a heavy sword, going toe to toe with the giant.

He refused.

He chose to do something that was really stupid from an onlooker's perspective: to fight with a slingshot and five stones.

Nobody had *ever* defeated a giant like that, let alone a young, inexperienced shepherd.

Yet he chose the sling, which was what he was *really good* at.

The story of David and Goliath has made it through thousands of years of history because of an undercelebrated fact: David defeated the giant *his* way.

This has a hell of a lot more to do with you and your business than you may think. In fact, you need to say "Screw it!" to the traditional business advice the B.S. hacks and gurus try to sell you.

Instead, slay your Goliath with these five stones.

FIVE STONES

1. YOU DON'T NEED FUNDING.

You need one customer. Go sell one person your product, idea, or service, and see how they like it. That's all you need to start a business. Don't listen to anyone who says there are limited ways to fund yourself. There are 5,000 ways to fund a company and 6,790 different structures. This is how Gravy did it for years.

2. YOU DON'T HAVE TO DO YOUR HIRING LIKE ANYONE ELSE.

People are going to tell you how you need to "structure" to hire people. The people you don't hire are going to tell you why you are doing it wrong. The recruiters are going to tell you why your pay isn't where it needs to be. Listen, but don't let it bother you. Do it your way.

3. YOU DON'T HAVE TO MARKET THE SAME WAY AS EVERYONE ELSE.

Be like King David, and do what you are good at. At Gravy, right now we are the best at relational marketing. We connect with people in personalized ways and do lots of video prospecting. Consultants tell us we should market differently, and we certainly learn from consultants. However, it's your life on the line with Goliath. Do your marketing your way.

4. YOU DON'T HAVE TO SELL THE WAY EVERYONE ELSE DOES.

People told us, "Nobody will sign a twelve-month contract with your company." Not true. We have scaled with twelve-month contracts. We want to scare off the people who aren't committed to making this partnership work, and a twelve-month contract does that really well!

Our churn is so much lower than our competitors' because of this decision. Sure, we lose deals, but not too many.

Our way works for us. What's your way?

5. DO WHAT MATCHES YOUR OWNER'S INTENT.

I spent so much time in my last companies trying to be like other companies. It's truly maddening if you consider all the ways you can build something. As you grow, you are going to question everything. Don't.

Your secret sauce is picking your unique way to attack the market. People will tell you to be bigger or smaller or that you need to structure one way or another.

Just be you. This sounds obvious, but it took me fourteen years to arrive at the point of being comfortable in my own skin and with my leadership style.

Here's are the four practical slings for me.

FOUR SLINGS

1. TIME (WHITE SPACE)

I've tried so many time management systems, and I hate them all. Seventy percent of my calendar is white space. Sounds irresponsible, right? Wrong. I'm a creative, and my best ideas come in the white space; they don't come during meetings.

I've chosen to have a loose calendar because that's my slingshot. When my calendar is busy, I'm not effective.

You may consider me lazy now; however, my superpower comes through managing my *energy* more than my time. My energy wanes when I'm busy.

2. TIME MANAGEMENT (PARTNER)

I don't manage anyone. The CEO usually has direct management reports. Not I. I have exactly zero. Renee, my Gravy co-founder and chief of staff, does all the management.

Look, like I know I need white space, I know I have no business managing anyone. All I would do is frustrate them and myself. (Remember that self-awareness piece? It's crucial here too.) So I just don't do it. I work with other people who do. If you want, you can do the same thing!

3. RECRUITING (LINKEDIN)

In case you're wondering what I do with all my white space, one of my jobs is recruiting talent to Gravy. Again, I do this differently. Instead of using recruiters and personal networks, I've built a healthy, engaged LinkedIn following.

I spend a large amount of time writing for and connecting with people on LinkedIn. This is the opposite of wasting a CEO's time.

And even if it is a waste of time, you already know my thought: I don't care.

Here is the benefit: we have a brand now where we can recruit amazing people quickly with no recruiter fees. That's a heck of a slingshot!

4. MEETING STRATEGY (SLACK)

I hate operational meetings. I like walking meetings, but I hate sitting around and talking about metrics and data. So I don't do many meetings. I love strategy meetings, so I reserve my time for those. I'm at my best in these.

But for everything else, if you can send it in a Slack message, why meet about it?

What armor and weapons are you using that don't fit? Who is telling you to hoist it anyway, even if it's going to get you killed?

Be like David and say, "Thanks for your advice, but hell no." Because you are the expert on your business. Not me. Not anyone else.

NO-B.S. HACKS

No-B.S. Hack 1: Trust your gut.

No-B.S. Hack 2: Live in the Results Economy.

No-B.S. Hack 3: Flush the toilet.

No-B.S. Hack 4: Retire now.

No-B.S. Hack 5: Pick up your slingshot and do it your way.

LET 'EM GO

You Don't Own "Your" People

You know what upsets me? When owners and CEOs say "*my* staff" or "*my* people." In case the people who speak this way aren't clear, let me cut through this B.S. way of thinking and say it.

Your staff aren't *yours.*

(Let's be honest: you probably wouldn't even want them.)

There's an inherent conceit in this language. You can say "my child" about your kids because you made them or adopted them, so you are *ultimately* responsible for them. But you can't say "my" when it comes to your staff.

The old-school way of thinking is that you control people and own them with a paycheck. This is over. Yet our vocabulary says a lot about what we truly think.

We still think we own people.

I speak with many owners who truly believe they can control their teams. They can't. Control is an illusion. The only things we control are our actions.

What angers me even more than a misplaced "my" is a major reason for people hating their lives at work. Want to know what it is? Two words: corporate terrorism.

You handcuff people with a salary and benefits, use them up, and get mad if they post on LinkedIn or do other things you can't control.

Then when they aren't serving you, you fire them. These are typically people showing up for their pay who have no life purpose. Miserable. It's not far from a scenario straight out of George Orwell's *1984*.

I feel irate when company leaders try to muzzle people and forbid them from building their own networks and brands to get better jobs.

At Gravy, we believe that real leaders help people leave a company better than they come in. We believe you should understand they never were, never are, and never will be "your people."

They are humans, and they have the right to a voice in the market.

Why don't they do what you want? Why don't they have enthusiasm for your work? Because you think you own them, and they sense it. But they don't tell you off to your face because they are scared to lose that paycheck you dangle over their heads.

For all the corporate terrorists reading this book, there's a better way. You can regain your humanity and unlock the full potential of your company's Mission, Vision, and Purpose.

It starts with removing the handcuffs from "your people." Unlatch the muzzle, and let them speak up and speak out.

Now, let's get practical.

TELL ME WHAT YOU WANT— WHAT YOU REALLY, REALLY WANT

When people join Gravy and we ask them to identify their Aspirational Intent, we aren't scared of *any* answer. It's far better to be real and not hide; then we can truly help each other.

I had a guy tell me a few weeks ago that Gravy is a stepping-stone on his way to becoming a VP. I loved his answer because it was honest. Plus, I can help him get there. I'm fine being whatever he wants us to be, as long as he performs well and plays nice with others while he's here.

The fact is, people go to work for different reasons. I had a woman tell me, "I work here because I was bored. This gives me something to do that isn't boring."

That's a damn fine answer.

I have *many* who say, "I came to work with you so I could learn how to be an entrepreneur. I want to start my own business one day."

This is *awesome*!

A dream of mine is to create an entrepreneurial tree. Just like a family tree, I want to grow seven companies from Gravy's team members. I want to see them do amazing things. Not only that, but I hope I can be their first investor!

You get the most out of people by giving them the most:

- Helping them.
- Connecting them.
- Believing in them.

At your company, you will unlock their purpose and fulfill their desires. It's why they are showing up! Instead of trying to lord your paycheck over them, you will celebrate their personal success.

NO-B.S. HACKS

No-B.S. Hack 1: Trust your gut.

No-B.S. Hack 2: Live in the Results Economy.

No-B.S. Hack 3: Flush the toilet.

No-B.S. Hack 4: Retire now.

No-B.S. Hack 5: Pick up your slingshot and do it your way.

No-B.S. Hack 6: Free the people and watch them soar.

DECADE OF DESTINY

Leave Them Better than They Came In

Each person in your organization has way more on their mind than how to work their very best at your company.

That "pressing issue" rubs shoulders with things like:

- Student loans
- Bills
- Rent
- Mortgage
- Taxes
- Tickets
- Career goals
- Relationship issues
- Kids
- Sick kids

- Teens
- Angry teens
- The DMV
- Retirement
- Aging parents
- Physical health
- Personal growth
- Spirituality
- Legacy

All this and more. Plus, every person is asking themselves, *How am I doing? How am I feeling right now?*

You're less important than you think, boss. However, you, your company, and the work and lifestyle you provide *are* an important element. You're rattling around in the head of every person connected to your business.

So here is the principle I'm deriving from this, which I believe to be true: everything affects everything.

Simply put, everything connects. You can try to segment life, but as I like to say, *life leaks*. The good from one issue leaks into the other issues. The bad from one issue does the same.

It's the butterfly effect. But I don't care about a thousand miles away. I care about right here, right now.

Within our own lives, and within your organization, life is leaking. It's dripping and making ripples that matter. We have to understand the holistic nature of the human beings we work alongside.

Once you deeply understand that every team member is a *whole person* and everything connects, you can offer this *whole person* truly great compensation. Your team member can get a paycheck anywhere. The question is: why will they want to get one from you and your company?

The greatest benefits aren't medical benefits or 401(k)s. While those things are good and necessary, Gallup Chairman and CEO Jim Clifton reported that 85 percent of people still hate their jobs because owners focus on the people's *work* more than on their *worth*. Namely, their *well-being*. ("The World's Broken Workplace." https://news.gallup.com/opinion/chairman/212045/world-broken-workplace.aspx.)

I know. I did this, too, for about twelve years.

So how did I figure out what *is* truly great compensation?

I stared into the crystal ball of my Owner's Intent and asked, "If my kids work here, what will I want Gravy to help them with?"

The answer was simple: life. All of it because *everything affects everything*.

Which means you—employer, entrepreneur, colleague—*can* affect *everything* in your team members', contractors', and colleagues' lives. Your role is far deeper than you thought. This is why I think the greatest benefit Gravy can offer *is not* monetary compensation; it's providing growth opportunities that will benefit team members for the rest of their lives.

This keeps me awake some nights, thinking about how we can provide development and opportunities that make our people better.

During their onboarding at Gravy, we tell people, "Our goal is for you to leave better than you came in."

We continue to say it, and I hear our team members saying it constantly. I know it's a statement that becomes more real with repetition.

Now, here's the mind trash of a business owner: *If I'm being honest, I didn't want to type that bit about "leaving you better," because I know there will be people who read this book who will say, "Yeah right, Casey, you liar. You say that but don't live up to it."*

I'm tempted to believe this mind trash because I don't always get it right.

Gravy doesn't always get it right either, but that doesn't stop us from taking tangible steps toward it—one decade at a time.

DECADE OF DESTINY

While thinking about the goal of making Gravy's team members' lives better (which means I was thinking using my Owner's Intent), I asked, "How can we help each team member in the areas of life that matter most?"

Our best answer was to devise a full-life planning system to help each Gravy team member create a personal Life Intent. Inventing this system was a big deal. It took our team 2.5 days at an in-person summit. It's what every high school, college, and business should offer but usually doesn't.

It's called Decade of Destiny. We begin with this: "Fast-forward your life ten years into the future. If you had to write the story in advance, what would your life look like?"

We call this Vivid Vision. We help each team member write their story. They think about their relationships. They imagine the ages of their kids. They think through their money, health, and well-being. They create an image of their preferred futures.

Like my pastor Andy Stanley says, "You are going to end up somewhere. You might as well end up there on purpose."

They think through three main areas of life that we would all like to improve over the next ten years:

FULFILLED RELATIONSHIPS

Most human beings want to be intimately loved. We want to experience meaningful friendships and spirituality or faith.

I always say that if your relationships are messed up, *everything* feels messed up. So we have every team member write a detailed story of their preferred future relationships and the fulfillment they want.

EXPONENTIAL ENERGY

Who wants to get into their future and lack the energy and health to enjoy life to the full?

My friend David always says, "I want to die healthy."

This is what we talk about with our team. What would it look like physically, mentally, and emotionally to show up in ten years full of passion and vigor for life? They write this story. They imagine living a life full of energy.

COMPOUNDING WEALTH

Most people are very worried about their finances. Money is connected to our hearts; having enough money is like having enough love. You need both to go on living.

Some of the worst stress I've ever felt has been financial stress. I'm sure you've felt the same. It's like you're carrying barbell weights on your back while a boa constrictor twists around your guts.

So we don't ignore this. We push our team to think through the career they want, at whatever company:

- We ask them to think about the salary they'll make.
- We inspire them to think about their investments, short-term and long-term.
- We get them fired up about starting their own company one day.

Last but not least, we have them plan out their generosity. Very few people look back and wish they'd given less. In fact, the money that charitable people give away is sometimes the only money they consider perfectly spent. We help them make a plan to become charitable people.

Want to do your own Decade of Destiny? Gravy ain't greedy.
We have all of our Decade of Destiny materials located at
dontfail.biz/destiny.

DECADE OF DESTINY

Fulfilled Relationships	Exponential Energy	Compounding Wealth
Family	Mental	Professional
Friends	Emotional	Investments
Faith	Physical	Giving

When our team members talk about Gravy to their friends, they talk about this program more than the company.

For a decade, I've published a schedule of the dates we will gather every quarter to focus on achieving our Decade of Destiny plans together. Everyone is welcome, even after leaving Gravy.

It's my contribution to helping them leave Gravy better than they came in and excel in life. I want them to get to the end of their next decade and not tell the story of some company that was doing payment recovery.

I want them to tell their story.

LAURA'S STORY

Laura and her husband have two beautiful children.

Their son was diagnosed with autism when Laura was in her early days at Gravy. She called Renee and told her as soon she found out. They shared tears as Laura invited us into her family's story.

She was frightened at first, not knowing what the future would hold. Lots of unknowns.

But through Decade of Destiny, she created a plan for what the best life for her son would be. She wrote down her dream that he would have the best help available. During her journey, she found out that Jacksonville, Florida, has amazing resources.

She spent the first year of her decade focusing on getting financially free so they could one day move to Jacksonville.

As of right now, they are in the middle of making that move. She sent me a note with this story, and it's what I would want for my adult daughter: a company that cares about her.

Laura won't work here forever, but she will forever remember Gravy's impact.

JESSICA'S STORY

I got a text yesterday from a woman named Jessica.

She had a lot of student loans and was starting her career at Gravy. As she went through Decade of Destiny, she made some tough decisions to get out of debt—fast.

She texted me, "Hey, here is a bright spot for you today: You have accelerated my financial freedom, and I just paid off one of my three private student loans. I'm on track to pay off the other two by the end of the year because of Gravy."

ONE MOTHER'S STORY

I met with a woman yesterday who isn't just new to Gravy; she's newly married and has a new baby too. She has buried herself in the enormous tasks of working motherhood. Decade of Destiny gave her an incredible opportunity to stop her runaway train and *think*. As she considered the coming decade, she decided she wants to be mentally and emotionally healthy.

In our conversation she revealed to me that she was planning to start seeing a professional counselor, taking dance lessons, and reading books on mental health. I am 100 percent in favor of her awesome choices and the choices of so many other Decade of Destiny alums.

You see, great culture happens when you help people live great lives. Great work happens when people *feel* great. Help team members get what they want out of life, and you will have no problem getting what you want out of business. *It's all connected.*

NO-B.S. HACKS

No-B.S. Hack 1: Trust your gut.

No-B.S. Hack 2: Live in the Results Economy.

No-B.S. Hack 3: Flush the toilet.

No-B.S. Hack 4: Retire now.

No-B.S. Hack 5: Pick up your slingshot and do it your way.

No-B.S. Hack 6: Free the people and watch them soar.

No-B.S. Hack 7: Everything affects everything.

Chapter 3.8

GIVE A DAMN

How Caring Is a Strategic Advantage

I'm amazed at how many companies say they care about their clients and teams, but when they're actually in need, the company doesn't show up. To stand out in the market there's a simple thing you can do, which is what I call *giving a damn*.

That's why we have a Gravy Cares system. If you ever want to send a care package or gift to anyone, just do it. Gravy will reimburse you.

I think about one of my favorite humans, Erin. Her daughter fell at preschool and gashed her head open. It was a really bad accident. One of our team members sprang into action and had an oversized stuffed animal and tons of candy and flowers on Erin's front porch before her daughter returned from the ER.

Because we operate with a team-first mindset, we want to care for the whole person, including the person's family. Nobody ever forgets genuine gestures like this.

We also love good news. That's why we follow our clients online. When we see celebratory life moments, such as a new baby, a graduation, and so on, we immediately send care packages.

We don't skimp here, either. We load them up with fun things, including a "Gravy Baby" onesie.

(You wouldn't believe how few companies do this simple act of caring. Ever seen a "Microsoft Baby" or "Tesla Baby"? I don't think so. They send an Instagram "congratulations!" instead of giving a damn.)

RELATIONAL CURRENCY

Nothing has built a more human relationship to our team and clients than showing up in life.

We believe in this so much that we have designed an actual process around it.

SHOW UP FIRST

Everyone remembers firsts. We want the team to *instantly* drop everything they are doing and take care of clients and people.

If someone is in the hospital, show up first. Even if you can't get in, nobody will ever forget it.

SHOW UP PERSONALLY

We don't send canned gifts. We make sure everything is personalized. We send more handwritten notes to the team and clients than anyone I know.

Don't do canned stuff. Show that you care for the person by making it personal.

The number one way to do this is to say their name. "Elizabeth, I hope this oversized teddy bear helps your head feel better."

That will make a mom's heart explode with love and care.

SHOW UP GENEROUSLY

Take care of people, even if it stretches you financially.

At the end of your life, you will not wish you'd skimped on giving a damn about people in life's pivotal situations.

If you are the company owner, pay for it all. Nothing matters more than our team, clients, and people in and around our companies.

At Gravy, we have made the conscious decision to provide budget for each team member to care for each other, in addition to random acts of kindness we execute as a group.

During Thanksgiving 2020, for instance, we gave each team member twenty-five dollars on their paycheck to show generosity toward someone in their lives. I don't say this to brag—I want to show you how you can remove the B.S. theory about care and making it something practical.

I do this because—you guessed it—this is what I would want my children's company to do.

NO-B.S. HACKS

No-B.S. Hack 1: Trust your gut.

No-B.S. Hack 2: Live in the Results Economy.

No-B.S. Hack 3: Flush the toilet.

No-B.S. Hack 4: Retire now.

No-B.S. Hack 5: Pick up your slingshot and do it your way.

No-B.S. Hack 6: Free the people and watch them soar.

No-B.S. Hack 7: Everything affects everything.

No-B.S. Hack 8: Give a damn about people.

LET FREEDOM RING

Give Everybody What They Want

I received a tour of my friend's office. His company went from nothing to an acquisition by Target for $550 million in just three years.

I was so curious to learn more about that kind of speed. How in the hell do you grow that fast? I asked my friend, and his answer was not what I expected.

He said, "We give everybody everything they want."

"What do you mean?" I asked.

"I'll show you." He took me to a corner in the building with a reading nook and coloring books everywhere. I thought it was for kids. It wasn't.

"The environment was stressful," he said. "But people were saying that if they had adult coloring books, they'd be able to do their jobs better. So the next week, they installed an adult coloring book station."

That's just the beginning.

In the middle of the office is a full bar. A lot of people said they wished they could get to know others better because the company was growing so fast. They said that going to a bar after work wasn't feasible because of family priorities.

So they installed a fully stocked bar in the office.

Then he took me to a computer and said, "Watch this."

He opened Slack, and there were crazy channels like "Cat Lovers." *Cats?* I thought. *On the company's Slack?* It seemed out of place at work. But that was just the beginning. There was a channel where team members told the founder about their hobbies, and I said, "This is a dumbass idea."

People were saying and creating whatever they wanted. Beyond the boundaries of what even *I* thought work was supposed to be.

My friend then said something that forever changed my approach to leadership: "Give people whatever they want because it will cost you more to fight it."

This wasn't about what was appropriate. This was about freedom.

The driving question at this company isn't "What will freedom destroy?" Rather, it's "What will freedom *create?*"

When people know their boss will say, "Sure, do that," they won't even ask her. They'll just do it. I like that: fewer questions, more action. And by now you know how I feel about management.

So we adopted it at Gravy. Honestly, I had no idea how powerful it would be. We created freedom not only to have what you want at Gravy, but to *be* who you want. Freedom to decide what you want to decide. Because *you* matter.

My friend with the Target-acquired company dug deeper into the coloring books.

"They rarely get used. What's the point, then?" he continued. "The woman who asked for them was extremely grateful to be listened to, and she crushes her job. Listening to an employee like this is the cheapest productivity hack in the world."

Spend $100 on coloring books, and you've allowed someone to be happy because she is *heard*.

Just ask yourself who you go to bat for: the person who doesn't care about you, or the person who *does*? Same holds true with a colleague, manager, or boss.

He mentioned the bar and said it gets used less than you'd think. "It's great. If people want to get drunk at work and not get their work done, that's on them. They have visible metrics. If the person can't *not* drink, they will miss their metrics and get fired."

"We make it free speech and model respect," he said about Slack, "but we don't try to restrict what's said or created."

Today at Gravy, thanks in part to my tour of this incredibly fast startup, we now give people ultimate freedom.

They have a budget and metrics. Everything is tied to results and relationships. So if you want to be a rapper on the job, like KZ, who works for us, do it. If you want to have a company 5K run, go for it. Lead it. Want fifty coffee mugs that say Gravy? We will buy them. Need two computer screens? Absolutely.

This creates a fun company. This creates a group of people empowered to know each other and care about each other. This accelerates freedom inside work *and* outside it.

GETTING PERSONAL

Our biggest version of this freedom is helping people build their personal brands on LinkedIn. A lot of people want to build a brand just so they can command a higher salary or get the dream job they want.

Not at Gravy.

We actually teach them how to leverage LinkedIn so they can develop their own personalities and voices. They can do and say whatever they want. They can say good or bad about us. We don't try to control any of it.

We've had a lot of new hires even in the past year that are coming to Gravy as their first job out of college. Their first job! That's a huge deal to me and to our team. When I think about those team members, the biggest value we can add to them is not to teach them more skills. It's to teach them the value they bring to the marketplace on LinkedIn.

Casey, Erik, Dharma, Patience, Taylor—these are only a few of the names of team members who have become known on LinkedIn for their perspective and unique position in the world.

Remember, we don't try to control any of it because it's about *their* voice, not *ours*. This is only surprising because too many owners are dictators (remember corporate terrorism?). They try to control it *all*. Those owners are stress balls of misery.

Free the people!

The speed of our company requires us to let people have and do what they want. There's still accountability. If people make bad decisions over and over, I fire them. But we use visible metrics and let those be the guide—not an artificial status quo.

Quit wasting your time trying to control your people. Just give them what they want—coloring books, a bar, or maybe even a cat Slack channel.

Here's what I've found. They won't always use it when you give it to them because the coloring books, the bar, or even the Slack channel isn't at the core of what they wanted.

What they wanted, really wanted, all along is knowing you care.

NO-B.S. HACKS

No-B.S. Hack 1: Trust your gut.

No-B.S. Hack 2: Live in the Results Economy.

No-B.S. Hack 3: Flush the toilet.

No-B.S. Hack 4: Retire now.

No-B.S. Hack 5: Pick up your slingshot and do it your way.

No-B.S. Hack 6: Free the people and watch them soar.

No-B.S. Hack 7: Everything affects everything.

No-B.S. Hack 8: Give a damn about people.

No-B.S. Hack 9: Give everybody what they want.

READY OR NOT, HERE THEY COME

(Don't) Table that Promotion

Having a college education matters zero for working at Gravy.

We believe in hiring to Core Values and then giving people a shot to do things. Our head of technology didn't finish college and is a wizard.

Some of our more recent college grads are instantly promoted to leadership positions because we believe in giving people a shot.

The best way for adults to grow is to have a real-world project or a role. A lot of you reading this take yourselves and your companies *so seriously* that you are limiting the potential of both. You won't just give people a shot.

We believe in inviting people to the table *before they think they are ready* and giving it a go. That's why we've given them a framework to do it on the job.

THE 4 TABLES OF GRAVY

It's called the "4 Tables of Gravy." Everyone is on a Table (level of the organization), and it is a special invite to join our team.

4 Tables of Gravy

	WHO	WHY	WHEN
EXECUTIVE TABLE	C-Suite/SVP	99% Strategy	2x per month Thursdays, 10:00am
LEADERSHIP TABLE	VP/Sr Director	80% Strategy 20% Ops	2x per month Thursdays, 10:00am
MANAGEMENT TABLE	Director/Manager	Leadership Development	1x per month Tuesdays, 11:00am
ALL TEAM	Individual Contributors	Personal Development	3x per month Tuesdays, 11:00am

Within the 4 Tables of Gravy are the five principles that guide our invitations:

1. IT'S A *PRIVILEGE.*

We approach our seats with honor. I'm proud to be at the table and show mutual respect for others at the table.

2. IT'S A *RESPONSIBILITY.*

We let people know that when you sit at the table, you carry weight. As I write this, I feel the weight today of ninety-one mortgage payments of our team members. When I see team members, I see their kids and families.

When we sit at the table, we see whole people because *everything affects everything* (remember?). This responsibility drives me to lead responsibly.

3. IT'S ABOUT *RESULTS.*

When we sit at the table, we bring our leadership results first and our opinions second. You are only as successful as your team.

We never blame the team for our lack of results. When we win, the team gets credit. When we lose, I own 100 percent of the blame.

Being 100 percent responsible is real leadership, even as that leadership is reflected and tested by how well the team performs.

4. IT'S ABOUT *RELATIONSHIPS.*

At work, you need to build a table of people who want to eat together. In a virtual world, we must spend a lot of time beyond the work to know people as humans.

Our temptation will be to skip this to "get the work done," but the greatest work of leadership is relationships. Out of relationships, trust is built. Out of trust, full potential is reached.

5. IT'S *NOT GUARANTEED.*

You don't *own* your seat at the table. All seats are *rented* based on the results and relationships of our teams. Rent is due daily, weekly, and monthly. Just because you are at the table doesn't mean you will stay at the table.

Also, we might hire your future boss at the table. Or you might become the boss at the table. As Gravy grows, you must grow, and I must grow.

ALICIA'S STORY

Speaking of growth, let me tell you a story that involves a toilet. Yes, a toilet.

Alicia had been out of work for seven years before starting at Gravy. She took some time off to be a stay-at-home mom (and a kick-ass one at that). Her last text to her husband before applying to work at Gravy stated, "You do complex analyses that affect the future of your company and its employees. I conquer toilet stains."

Alicia had no idea that years later, she would be sitting at the executive table at Gravy. She has had over ten titles within our company, and I'm sure her current one won't be her last. Alicia demonstrates how important it is to *work* to earn your seat and *work* to keep it.

TABLE IT

The quality of the lives in our company rests in the hands of the people at the 4 Tables.

King Arthur had one; we have four. We each sought to ensure effective leadership through the voices, results, and opinions of those invited to sit at the table.

In my experience, I've found that the best table members are those who consistently approach their seat with humility, knowing every day is a chance to prove their worthiness of having an invitation.

I've also hired very talented people who thought they deserved to be at the table and were horrible to work with. Sure, they may have been geniuses; I just don't want to spend my time at the table with people I don't enjoy being around. And neither should you.

So invite carefully, thoughtfully, and wisely. But resolve to invite others in and give people a shot *before* they are ready.

Creating a Table system at your organization so people can have a pathway for more leadership isn't just the wise thing to do; it's one of the most effective things you can do. I highly, highly recommend you get to work at creating this today.

NO-B.S. HACKS

No-B.S. Hack 1: Trust your gut.

No-B.S. Hack 2: Live in the Results Economy.

No-B.S. Hack 3: Flush the toilet.

No-B.S. Hack 4: Retire now.

No-B.S. Hack 5: Pick up your slingshot and do it your way.

No-B.S. Hack 6: Free the people and watch them soar.

No-B.S. Hack 7: Everything affects everything.

No-B.S. Hack 8: Give a damn about people.

No-B.S. Hack 9: Give everybody what they want.

No-B.S. Hack 10: (Don't) table the promotion.

Chapter 3.11

FAILEBRATION

Celebrating the Art of Screwing Up

Ray Dalio is one of the greatest investors in the history of the world. He shared a story in his book *Principles* that changed my life and Gravy's leadership.

One of his young fund managers made some irresponsible trades with a high price tag.

The guy ended up losing over $1 million.

Ray wrote about this manager's inner turmoil. He thought that his loss was too big to recover from, and he despaired over how to handle it and keep his reputation, let alone his job.

Often, when we mess up, we try to cover it up. We feel the shame and want to hide. Knowing this fact of human nature, Ray always told his people, "I will never get mad at you for a mistake, but I will fire you for hiding it."

The manager walked into Ray's office and shared the news of his million-dollar loss.

Ray looked at him and said, "Because you admitted your failure fast and honestly, we will look at this as your master's degree in trading. What did you learn?"

Wow!

Ray wrote that he became one of his best managers.

The lesson for me is this: how you treat people when they mess up *defines your culture* more than anything else you do from this book. When you mess up or they do, how do you handle it?

We took Ray's story to heart by creating a culture of celebrating failures instead of punishing them.

One of the ways we did this was by creating a Slack channel called #failebration."

This channel is full of fails from life and work. But bigger than that are the stories of owning mistakes openly and fast—the actual point.

One of Gravy's client managers was doing an onboarding call. The client asked for something more expensive than what we had in the contract, and she verbally agreed, but the contract was never updated. So we made the client more money, and the client was supposed to pay us more money than the contract specified.

Well, a few months later, the client pulled out Gravy's contract and said they wouldn't pay us.

It was close to $20,000.

Our mistake was failing to change the contract when the client asked us to change our process. Gravy was rightly owed the $20,000. But the contract didn't reflect that.

I called the client manager responsible into a meeting. I remember it like it was yesterday. She proceeded to tell us the entire story. She didn't cover it up or make excuses. She 100 percent *owned* the error.

As she told the story, she looked like she was about to cry. I told her that because she owned the mistake, we were going to consider this her master's degree in client management paid for by Gravy.

She ended up receiving the MVP Award, our highest honor, which we give away two times a year.

Inside our Slack channel, we see daily examples of big and small fails, and it's a reminder of one of our five Core Values: "We don't take ourselves too seriously."

There is rarely a failure that's not recoverable.

Now to take this a bit further, if you don't do anything else I say to do in this book, do this: cover your people. Always.

If they mess up something publicly, you take the blame personally. If they miss the sales goal, you take the blame and communicate it to everyone that it was your fault.

Believe the best in the team *first,* and cover them from any shame or embarrassment. Nothing will serve you better over the long haul than this.

This especially matters to me because of my Owner's Intent: how do I want my adult children to be treated *when* they mess up at work?

I want them to be celebrated for admitting their failures and then covered by their leaders *when* they do.

I see too many bosses passing the blame—and the buck—and this is total B.S. You will destroy your culture, credibility, and future.

Cover your people. It will always be the right thing to do today.

Plus, you never know when you might need them to cover you tomorrow.

NO-B.S. HACKS

No-B.S. Hack 1: Trust your gut.

No-B.S. Hack 2: Live in the Results Economy.

No-B.S. Hack 3: Flush the toilet.

No-B.S. Hack 4: Retire now.

No-B.S. Hack 5: Pick up your slingshot and do it your way.

No-B.S. Hack 6: Free the people and watch them soar.

No-B.S. Hack 7: Everything affects everything.

No-B.S. Hack 8: Give a damn about people.

No-B.S. Hack 9: Give everybody what they want.

No-B.S. Hack 10: (Don't) table the promotion.

No-B.S. Hack 11: Cover your people.

WORK HARD, PLAY HARDER

Culture-Building Rituals

Have you ever noticed that our lives are centered around rituals? Holidays, family vacations, daily routines, everything we do follows a stream of regularly scheduled practices and events.

Even though I'm a free spirit, I thrive on the rituals in culture and in my life personally. Let me tell you about some of my favorite.

As a boy from Alabama, I live for Alabama football. I always tell my wife that I will be fully reliable and available every day of the year except on Alabama football game days. I'll still be present, just a little distracted. (Actually that's B.S., I'm 100 percent distracted.)

Anyway, before football season every year, I get together with a couple of my close friends, and we prep. We talk about the players, the coach, the performance, the competition—anything and everything related to the game. It's become one of my favorite days of the entire year. A ritual I always look forward to.

My family has a pretty set schedule of rituals as well. We have yearly trips we always take together, in addition to individual trips with my son and daughter for one-on-one time. These dates are etched into the calendar each year and have become some of the greatest landmarks in my life.

That's what rituals do—they etch landmarks in your life. They create a pause in time, a moment where you can look back and look forward.

Remember, rituals are where culture is built. Culture for your family, friend groups, and work teams.

That's why at Gravy, we decided to build a modern company guided by rituals. (Okay, before you tune out, stick with me.)

I'm going to take you on a journey that includes each building block and why we do it. The point isn't for you to copy us; rather, it's to use these as inspiration for creating your own rituals that reinforce what *you* want.

Even if your Owner's Intent doesn't demand this, do it anyway. Everyone can create a more meaningful life through following these ideas.

ANNUAL SUMMIT

We host an annual summit for our full team. It's the most expensive investment we make as a company. We fly people to amazing places, and we stop working for 2.5 days.

This is time spent together, not working on the business, but working on ourselves.

We spend all year focused on doing business. We use these 2.5 days to:

- Build up the team.
- Learn from external and internal speakers who add value.
- Meet with our teams to build relationships.
- Eat, drink, and be merry, of course!

It's basically a summer camp for adults. Everyone looks forward to it so much. It's the highlight of our year.

At Summit, we give awards. This might be my favorite part.

- Five Core Value Awards
- Partner of the Year Award
- Client of the Year Award
- Revenue Velocity Award (This award comes with a real wrestling belt. And, yes, it's awesome.)
- MVP (Remember who got that? The person who owned her mistake.)

This is how we start off our summit, and everyone loves it! The previous award winners present. People share stories. It's an incredibly impactful experience that sets the tone for the rest of the time.

We invest 2 percent of our annual budget into this event. We have taken team Gravy to Cancun, Miami, Atlanta, and Nashville.

We plan to keep doing these amazing trips because of one question—you know by now! "How would I want my kids' company to celebrate and build them?"

Our annual summit is how.

GRAVY BIRTHDAY

Every May we bring our leadership team to a special location for a one-to-two-day celebration of Gravy's origin story. We celebrate our company's birthday. We take the time to pause, remember, and be grateful.

It's an annual reminder of where we came from.

We look back and tell the origin story of how and why Gravy started. We ask people to reflect on their growth with the company, both the trials and their stories.

Gravy Birthday is always a blast.

For example, one ritual on Gravy Birthday is to count how many clients we've added during the year, and then we toast to that number.

We give away gag gifts and have a lot of fun. It's a good ritual because everyone who attends always leaves feeling part of the Gravy story.

ALL-TEAM MEETINGS (A.K.A. GRAVY CHURCH)

We believe meetings should be about inspiration, not information. If it's information, send an email or Slack. But for inspiration, nothing replaces being there in person. So three times a month on Tuesdays, we bring our entire team together.

It started with two people. We're at eighty-three as I write this. We do it weekly.

If you added up how much those eighty-three hours are costing Gravy, you'd see that it's the most expensive hour of our week. The wisdom behind holding a $3,000-plus meeting three times a month is because Gravy is a leadership development company disguised as a payment recovery company.

During that hour (really, eighty-three hours):

- We teach leadership.
- We inspire Vision.
- We help people grow in their lives.
- We bring in guest speakers.

We hope to make it the best hour of the week. Sometimes we succeed, and sometimes we fail. But more often than not, that hour is valuable.

People ask, "How is it *valuable*? My team members hate meetings."

Me too! I hate *information* meetings. Here's the link to Gravy Church, our weekly all-team meeting. Going to dontfail.biz/inspiration will give you access to the magic of an *inspiration* meeting—without an altar call.

Whether it's in person or virtual, the rhythm of our all-team meetings has made the biggest difference in reinforcing culture and unity. It's an official, anticipated time when we celebrate each other and share client stories and wins.

You don't have to do these rituals, but I will tell you they make the difference.

Make your calendar reinforce your culture. Even if you say that you care about the people in your company, if your calendar doesn't, you don't.

NO-B.S. HACKS

No-B.S. Hack 1: Trust your gut.

No-B.S. Hack 2: Live in the Results Economy.

No-B.S. Hack 3: Flush the toilet.

No-B.S. Hack 4: Retire now.

No-B.S. Hack 5: Pick up your slingshot and do it your way.

No-B.S. Hack 6: Free the people and watch them soar.

No-B.S. Hack 7: Everything affects everything.

No-B.S. Hack 8: Give a damn about people.

No-B.S. Hack 9: Give everybody what they want.

No-B.S. Hack 10: (Don't) table the promotion.

No-B.S. Hack 11: Cover your people.

No-B.S. Hack 12: Instill culture-building rituals.

Chapter 3.13

SHHH*T SHOW

Don't Keep Secrets

I worked for a person early in my career who kept company numbers hidden. He had the right to do that, but it doesn't mean it was the right move.

Sometimes he was super stressed and said, "This is the most important month in the history of the company!" As a twenty-four-year-old, I interpreted that as, "I don't care if you have to work ninety hours. We will do this right now!"

I didn't know if we were in a season of opportunity or running out of money. I was controlled by the rhetoric of our fearful leader. It was traumatizing to work for him.

Money affects the leadership of any company, just like it affects every relationship and every person.

When things are tough, people get tense. The heat goes up. People are fired who usually wouldn't be. When things are good, everyone can feel the expanse open. The atmosphere is positive. There's camaraderie and a sense that we are unstoppable.

Money dictates a lot.

AN OPEN BOOK

Because of my negative experience working for someone who was leveraging debt he shouldn't have—and putting me under pressure in the process—I never want to do that to anyone at Gravy.

So we're an open book at Gravy. In fact, we have open books. We show everyone all the numbers. (Well, we do not share specific salaries, but we share everything else.)

Private business owners are called that for a reason. You don't owe an explanation to your team or clients. However, this secrecy comes with a cost I'm not willing to pay.

When the COVID-19 pandemic hit, we didn't know if we were going to go out of business or not. Our lives turned upside down. A few weeks into the world crisis, I got on the phone with seventeen team members, one by one, on a Sunday. I asked, "What's your number one fear right now?"

Some shared the fear that a family member would die.

But 90 percent of them said, "I'm scared I'm going to lose my job."

You can't operate in a crisis well *and* live under that fear. So we did something that we continue to do now—something that can help *your* team, whether or not you disclose your numbers.

We created a green, yellow, and red financial system:

- **Green**: Our sales and expenses are within 10 percent of budget month over month. Plus, we have a six-month cash reserve.
- **Yellow**: Our sales and expenses are off by 11 percent to 25 percent month over month. We are now biting into the six-month cash reserve.
- **Red**: Our sales and expenses are off by 26 percent or more. We've eaten three months of the cash reserves for all expenses.

What would have been unthinkable to my traumatizing boss was what we started to do during the pandemic. Every month, I updated the team on how we were doing and showed them the numbers.

Instead of causing upheaval, it gave clarity. You would not believe the amount of relief it brought to everyone. Also, you wouldn't believe the relief it brought to *me*.

As the CEO responsible for all those mortgages, I always felt like Gravy's leadership team and I were carrying a very heavy weight—in private. Now we could share it. By sharing our weight with more people, it got lighter. The team understood where the pressure was coming from. They understood the urgency.

We started operating with transparency and planning. We outlined the worst-case scenario and everything up to it so all of us knew what would happen if we didn't meet our benchmarks.

I've found that planning your finances this way is healthier for you and your team than just doing a dumbass pro forma that only shows the perfect scenario.

The pandemic was an extreme example. But being in business is always extreme.

Now we always create our budgets the green, yellow, and red way. We make plans in advance for what we'll do if we don't hit benchmarks.

It allows everyone to carry the weight, and it's easier to win together where others fail.

So many owners are worried about team member anger at how much profit the business is making. They are worried that people will think it's all about making the owner rich.

Well, if it is, it is. The team members will *feel* it is, whether they see it or not. So like we talked about in Part 1, just be brutally honest, and people will respect you. Then you won't carry the weight alone.

In typical, non-crisis times, we talk about numbers three to four times a year.

Overall, the principle is this: even if your finances are private, people will feel them in public.

NO-B.S. HACKS

No-B.S. Hack 1: Trust your gut.

No-B.S. Hack 2: Live in the Results Economy.

No-B.S. Hack 3: Flush the toilet.

No-B.S. Hack 4: Retire now.

No-B.S. Hack 5: Pick up your slingshot and do it your way.

No-B.S. Hack 6: Free the people and watch them soar.

No-B.S. Hack 7: Everything affects everything.

No-B.S. Hack 8: Give a damn about people.

No-B.S. Hack 9: Give everybody what they want.

No-B.S. Hack 10: (Don't) table the promotion.

No-B.S. Hack 11: Cover your people.

No-B.S. Hack 12: Instill culture-building rituals.

No-B.S. Hack 13: Open your books.

Chapter 3.14

ALL ABOARD!

Steal these Hiring and Recruiting Practices

People get mad when we talk about our hiring process. Here's my bottom line: would I want my kids to work for you?

HR people say, "Casey, that's not a good question because blah, blah, blah."

I don't care what HR thinks. I want to have people in the company who not only my kids would want to work for but who *I* want to work for.

Who wants people around who you look at and say, "I hope I never have to work for him"?

Well, why did you let him in the door in the first place? Because HR didn't ask my question.

And it's why most people hate work. Because they have a douche-bag boss or manager with an ego trip who wants nothing but to look good. The simplest way to make sure that never happens is not to hire a douchebag. Yet all of your fancy HR questions don't do that. My one question—which is about how you treat someone you love—always does.

Well, now you might be thinking, *This is a little strong, Casey. Are you an angry elf?*

No, I've just messed this up in my past. I want to save you the misery.

Here are two stats we are going to dig into:

- Gravy only hires A-plus players at $0 recruiting fees.
- Gravy only hires 0.02 percent of applicants.

The benefit of building a place my kids would want to work at is that I get to create a company that people love. For years to come, people who worked here will talk about Gravy with affection.

But this perk doesn't help recruit A-plus talent all the time.

So we have tapped into leveraging social media as the megaphone for attracting A-plus talent.

In fact, we train our team members to create their own personal brands online. We teach them how to be thought leaders in their personal areas of expertise.

The current medium we use to leverage this is LinkedIn.

THE MOST UNDERRATED SOCIAL NETWORK

A year ago, I didn't even know my LinkedIn password. A year ago, I thought LinkedIn was a place where unwelcomed messages flood your DMs of people wanting to "connect," a.k.a. sell you something you didn't actually need.

Once I got logged in, I realized LinkedIn wasn't about sales; it was a content platform. A place where people could add value to the marketplace and have organic reach *for free.*

At that moment, I decided to dive in. I paid someone way smarter than me to tell me how the LinkedIn algorithm works. I spent hours on this platform connecting with people, testing different types of content, and seeing what worked and what didn't.

Now it's my most-used platform. Why? Because you can grow your own personal brand and become known in the marketplace for your voice, all from posting content and knowing how you want to show up.

The LinkedIn algorithm is so favorable to content producers right now. Fun fact: there are eight hundred million people on LinkedIn, but according to content marketing agency Foundation, only 0.375 percent post weekly ("50+ LinkedIn Statistics Marketers Need to Know in 2021." https://foundationinc.co/lab/b2b-market ing-linkedin-stats.). So we teach our team to post almost daily!

The best part: as their personal brands grow, we grow! The *better* than best part: they get to keep their personal brands *forever* as assets for their own careers. Total win-win.

They don't have to do personal brand building, but a lot of them want to. They become leaders online, and it builds a massive influence for our company.

This matters because it breaks the branding chokehold of traditional leadership. (Here's that corporate terrorism again.)

We see so many leaders who try to control what is said about their companies that they only speak from their hallowed company pages. It's a mistake.

Activating your team to become raving fans online is the number one way to build your company brand. Suddenly, people will be knocking down virtual doors to simply get a shot at working for your company.

Team member testimonials can be faked. Personal LinkedIn posts can't be. People will be able to tell if you are forcing your people to post.

THE NEW SALES PIPELINE: RECRUITING

Everything we have talked about at work is now content people can write about online—to grow themselves and, in the process, grow the company. If you create a great company with wonderful people who share their experience online, you'll create an A-plus talent recruiting flywheel; it's simply the Law of Attraction at work.

The days of recruiters landing you some VP to pump up your brand from the inside out are over. It rarely works. What you want is someone who is less experienced but is following your company in the hopes of landing in that coveted 0.02 percent of hires.

As the leadership of your company, you have to create a recruiting pipeline just like you do a sales pipeline.

Here is the power of social recruiting: when we need candidates for anything, we just have to post it online. Then we get a slew of top candidates, ready and waiting.

It's true we love helping our team build their brands because it helps them and us. But you already know the reason under the reasons: it's what I want my kids' bosses to do for them.

Hey, HR folks, I know you're upset with me. You're probably thinking: *Enough with your stupid "what will you do for my kids?" question.*

I get it. It's not enough to simply *attract* top talent. We also want to ensure we allow the right people in the door.

To accomplish this, we have a process called the Gauntlet. (How do you like *that*, HR? Do I want my kids to run the Gauntlet? You bet I do.)

We learned this from a friend of mine called David Bonney. The tyrannical process includes:

- Five interviews (minimum)
- Role-playing
- Skills assessments
- Pilot projects
- Complete agreement from all stakeholders to hire the person.

And much more.

Honestly, I could write an entire section just on this. Instead, we have the entire hiring process available for download at dontfail. biz/people, along with explainers on how to use it.

The one thing you must know about this process is that it sucks. It's hard on the applicant. It's hard on us.

I'd like to think all applicants gain some experience and self-knowledge through the process, because it's less like normal hiring and more like Navy SEAL hell week.

However, when the chosen few make it through to the other side, they realize why our company has such a great culture that people post about online: it's because we only hire 0.02 percent of our applicants.

Whether your company is big or small, creating a recruiting engine doesn't start with HR. It starts with you.

It starts with how you create your Owner's Intent, how you build people and processes around this, and ultimately, how you treat your team, set them up, and set them *free*. Free to be their best selves, and free to share openly online with others. Others who in turn want to be their best selves, too, and see they can accomplish this within your company.

Build people internally and watch them build themselves—and your company—externally. This is Gravy's recipe for A-plus players and our not-so-secret hiring sauce you can steal and make your own.

NO-B.S. HACKS

No-B.S. Hack 1: Trust your gut.

No-B.S. Hack 2: Live in the Results Economy.

No-B.S. Hack 3: Flush the toilet.

No-B.S. Hack 4: Retire now.

No-B.S. Hack 5: Pick up your slingshot and do it your way.

No-B.S. Hack 6: Free the people and watch them soar.

No-B.S. Hack 7: Everything affects everything.

No-B.S. Hack 8: Give a damn about people.

No-B.S. Hack 9: Give everybody what they want.

No-B.S. Hack 10: (Don't) table the promotion.

No-B.S. Hack 11: Cover your people.

No-B.S. Hack 12: Instill culture-building rituals.

No-B.S. Hack 13: Open your books.

No-B.S. Hack 14: Leverage LinkedIn for recruiting and hiring
   A-plus players.

PART 4

NO-B.S. LEGACY

"The business of business is relationships.
The business of life is human
connection."

—Robin Sharma

When it comes to business, there will always be a never-quenched desire for *more*.

More targets. More growth. More revenue. More customers.

The same is true for life. There will always be more. But this *more* just hits differently.

More memories. More connections. More experiences. More relationships.

The hunger for *more* never ends, but the question we must ask ourselves each time this craving hits is: what is this costing me?

Rather, *who* is this costing me? Even if the "who" is, in fact, you.

More always comes at a price. As business owners—*as humans*—we must be ruthlessly honest when it comes to counting the cost of our business decisions.

And as you'll learn in this section, the stakes are simply too high to do otherwise.

Especially when what's at stake is your most precious commodity: your life and the lives of those closest to you.

Let's finish well.

Chapter 4.1

RESILIENCY

Winning after Failing

In 2008, when I started my first company, I had no idea what I was getting into. In fact, it sounds like a country song's lyrics. Here are a few highlights:

BEEN STOLEN FROM

FIRED FRIENDS AND RUINED RELATIONSHIPS

*ESCAPED A MURDER ATTEMPT IN ASIA WHILE TRYING TO SAVE
A COMPANY*

*BEEN DEFRAUDED BY A BUSINESS PARTNER WHO TOOK OUT A LINE
OF CREDIT I DIDN'T KNOW ABOUT, RAN IT UP, AND LEFT ME
TO PAY IT OFF*

HURT A MARRIAGE

LOST MILLIONS DURING DUE DILIGENCE

WORKED IN MY CLOSET THROUGHOUT THE NIGHT WHILE TRYING TO OUTSOURCE OPERATIONS TO THE PHILIPPINES

STARTED SEVENTEEN IDEAS IN THE LAST FOURTEEN YEARS THAT NEVER WENT ANYWHERE

LAID IN BED AT 3:00 A.M. WITH A BUDGET ON MY PHONE, FIGURING OUT HOW WE WOULD MAKE IT

BORROWED MONEY FROM FRIENDS AND PAID IT BACK UNDER PRESSURE

HIRED PEOPLE WHO WERE REALLY TERRIBLE FITS

FIRED SOME GOOD PEOPLE I COULDN'T PAY ANYMORE

HAD BUSINESS PARTNER BREAKUPS

BEEN MAD AT MYSELF FOR BEING GREEDY

NOT KNOWN WHY I EXIST ON THIS EARTH

DRANK MY BLUES AWAY A TIME OR TEN

SPENT MY LAST DOLLAR ON A TONY ROBBINS EVENT BECAUSE I WAS SO DESPERATE

Yet while business has been tough—to this point anyway—I've been tougher. It sounds egotistical, but I simply just don't ever want to quit on anything simply because it's *hard*.

I felt like my Papa quit on us when he took his life, and I want to right that wrong by living—and writing—my own redemption story. To redeem my mess. To redeem my tears.

While all this hardship and more is true, just like any good country song, there's always more to the story. In fact, I've also:

- Been married to my sweetheart wife for seventeen years
- Shown my kids what it's like to work hard
- Started four successful companies
- Sold three companies
- Built the house of my dreams
- Traveled the world
- Had the same group of best friends for twenty years
- Created hundreds of jobs for people to succeed in
- Originated some of the funniest stories to share at dinner tables
- Grown from some amazing mentors
- Lived fulfilled in understanding why I exist
- Gratefully enjoyed meaningful work
- Written this book
- My kids are both proud
- My wife is proud
- I am proud

Being proud is a new piece of my story. Until now, I've never felt proud of a company I've started. Today I can say I am. I'm proud of the stories. I'm proud of the culture. I'm proud of the people.

We have a lot left to accomplish. But as I write this, I write this with tears in my eyes. I'm proud. *(Remember that success barometer? It's also measured in tears. This one is overflowing.)*

I love you, Gravy. I love the journey paved with successes and failures that led me here.

My point is this: *hang in there.*

YOUR DECADE OF DESTINY

I'm thirteen years in and *just now* feeling proud of where I am. Everything great takes a decade to build. Get started today, and believe me when I tell you it's worth it.

It's worth it as long as you understand that you aren't building the company. Your company is building you.

I exist to create opportunity. And I will do so until my soul leaves my body.

In case you're curious about how my Owner's Intent ties into all this, my son, Gage, wears Gravy gear to school and loves to talk about it. My daughter, Darby, works for Gravy in the summer and is mentored by some of the women on our team.

Women she *loves* to work for.

Chapter 4.2

THE END—OR MAYBE THE BEGINNING?

My Obituary

Well, I just wrote thirty thousand words, and they told me I need to write more. Just like I skip introductions, I also skip conclusions.

But I won't skip my obituary.

As of now, you have my full, no-B.S. approach to business and life. But I've saved the best for last. I'm going to be brutally honest one more time because this is what *matters* most.

Let me say this straight: do not lay eaten up with cancer one day and wish you'd have loved people better. Both you and I are better than that.

As your life comes to an end—which it will, either today or on a day like today—you will regret making it all about money.

Remember in the beginning when I asked you to think about what stories people will tell at your funeral? Those stories are all defined by your Owner's Intent, Values, Mission, and Purpose and the way you *care* for people.

They all *matter*—not to your business, but to *you*. They define who you will be on your deathbed. Your whole life is about becoming the person you most want to be, and it all culminates in this singular moment when your party is over.

This doesn't just happen by accident. In order to get where you want to go and become who you want to be *on purpose*, it takes planning.

So I've already written my obituary. I suggest you do the same.

THE OBITUARY OF CASEY THOMAS GRAHAM

Casey Graham's life was full of passion, grace, generosity, adventure, and relationships. One of Casey's best friends said, "He was constantly creating experiences and memories that were mixed with meaningful depth and thrill-seeking adventure (and he usually picked up the tab). But the best part of him is that he loved me *no matter what*."

As an entrepreneur, Casey created many of the world's most amazing places for people to love what they did every day. Casey created companies so he could invest in people to become better versions of themselves. He famously said, "Business is boring, but people are fascinating. We create more businesses simply to know more people. People never get old, and I love creating places where people love to invest their most precious asset: time."

If you could see inside Casey's home, you would see a man who fiercely loved his family. His wife constantly said, "He treated me like a queen and went out of his way to help me see myself how God sees me. Fully known, fully loved. I felt secure in his arms."

His daughter, Darby, said, "I wish everyone in the world could have a daddy like mine. He was always there for me no matter what. I want to be just like him to my kids and grandkids."

His son, Gage, said, "The best part of my dad is he let me be me. He cared about me becoming the best version of myself. And he always said yes to a fishing trip with me."

Casey was known for taking in hurting friends, having the best parties at his farm, and going on the wildest adventures around the world. Everyone felt like they were his best friend because his motto was, "Treat everyone like they will become your best friend—and usually, they will."

Casey believed that depth with God was measured by how well you loved people. His love for the broken and hurting was evident. He was the go-to guy when someone needed a second chance. He believed in Jesus, and that was his only hope for life after death. The best part about him was that he didn't wait to experience eternal life; he experienced it on earth through his relationships.

THE STORIES THEY'LL TELL

Now it's your turn. From the beginning of this book, I promised you a real, raw, and honest view of business. From the highest of highs to the lowest of lows.

You also made a commitment to not lie to yourself while coming face-to-face with what you *really* want—from your business and from your life.

Just because our time is coming to a close doesn't mean this is the end. In fact, for you, it's truly just the beginning. So much so that the Intro bears revisiting here:

> You don't have to wait until the end of your life to realize you never became the person you wanted to be. In business. In life.
>
> This won't happen by accident or by chance. In order to win where others fail—in business and in life—you have to commit to getting rid of the B.S. garbage other books and gurus have been feeding you about getting rich, which always comes at the expense of other people.
>
> Because getting rich in business and being successful in life are two widely different things. Yet when done the right way, they actually can coexist. You can have the business success you want while also having the life you want.

So our journey toward your preferred future—toward getting what you *really* want—is going to end right back where it began, with one question:

What stories will be told about you at your funeral?

Think about it. *Really think about it.* Then let your obituary be your guide. Write yours now, and send it to me at dontfail.biz/obituary.

Obituaries and B.S. can't coexist. Only stories last. What stories are others going to tell about you at your funeral?

Only time will tell, but one thing is certain: I am going to write my story each day with intention. I invite you to do the same.

As you do, I'll leave you with one last thought:

Remember: no B.S. allowed.

I love you,

—CTG